The Guyer Girls

by Trisha Sugarek

Single copies of plays are sold for reading purposes only. The copying or duplicating of a play, or any part of play, by hand or by any other process, is an infringement of the copyright. Such infringement will be vigorously prosecuted.

Baker's Plays
7611 Sunset Blvd.
Los Angeles, CA 90042
bakersplays.com

NOTICE

This book is offered for sale at the price quoted only on the understanding that, if any additional copies of the whole or any part are necessary for its production, such additional copies will be purchased. The attention of all purchasers is directed to the following: this work is fully protected under the copyright laws of the United States of America, the British Commonwealth, including Canada, and all other countries of the Copyright Union. Violations of the Copyright Law are punishable by fine or imprisonment, or both. The copying or duplication of this work or any part of this work, by hand or by any process, is an infringement of the copyright and will be vigorously prosecuted.

This play may not be produced by amateurs or professionals for public or private performance without first submitting application for performing rights. Licensing fees are due on all performances whether for charity or gain, or whether admission is charged or not. Since performance of this play without the payment of the licensing fee renders anybody participating liable to severe penalties imposed by the law, anybody acting in this play should be sure, before doing so, that the licensing fee has been paid. Professional rights, reading rights, radio broadcasting, television and all mechanical rights, etc. are strictly reserved. Application for performing rights should be made directly to BAKER'S PLAYS.

No one shall commit or authorize any act or omission by which the copyright of, or the right to copyright, this play may be impaired. No one shall make any changes in this play for the purpose of production.

Publication of this play does not imply availability for performance. Both amateurs and professionals considering a production are strongly advised in their own interest to apply to Baker's Plays for written permission before starting rehearsals, advertising, or booking a theatre.

Whenever the play is produced, the author's name must be carried in all publicity, advertising and programs. Also, the following notice must appear on all printed programs, "Produced by special arrangement with Baker's Plays."

Licensing fees for THE GUYER GIRLS are based on a per performance rate and payable one week in advance of the production.

Please consult the Baker's Plays website at www.bakersplays.com or our current print catalogue for up to date licensing fee information.

Copyright © 2005 by Trisha Sugarek
Made in U.S.A.
All rights reserved.

Cover photos courtesy of Trisha Sugarek and the "Guyer Girls"

THE GUYER GIRLS
ISBN **978-0-87440-321-3**
#1727-B

For my mother, Violet, and all the Guyer Girls........

AUTHOR'S NOTES:

As a young child I never tired of the stories that my mother, Violet, told me about herself, Mama, and her six sisters, growing up in the back woods of Tumwater, Washington. All of the reminiscent stories told herein are true and I only took dramatic license to move the story along. The humor in the play is meant to come from the characters' personalities and antics. **MAMA**'s dialogue is more formal because she is a lady at the turn of the twentieth century. All the actors can transition to the second act with the exception of LaVerne who should be doublecast.

As generations pass, we are sadly losing the oral history of the American family. Every family has its' own rich and colorful tapestry of tales, history and characters.

Tell this story simply and honestly and your audience will embrace *The Guyer Girls*.

The author may be contacted through her publisher, **Baker's Plays.**

ACT I

Time: 1918
1920

Place: Mama's Kitchen,
Tumwater, Washington

ACT II

Time: 1941

Place: Mama's Kitchen,
Tumwater, Washington

CAST OF CHARACTERS

SOPHIA "MAMA"..........................The gentle matriarch of the Guyer family; she has raised thirteen children with love and compassion. With her husband, Levi, she migrated to America from France at the turn of the century [1900].

LILLAS................................The second oldest sister; she is 19 years old. She is the sensible one, and yet she gets pregnant at a time when a pregnant girl, unwed, was a family disgrace.

IVAH...................................The third sister; she is 17 and a hellion. She is the rebel of the family, constantly in trouble for her pranks and antics. She marries well but never loses her tomboy enthusiasm for mischief.

VIOLET............................The fourth sister; she is 16. Violet is a sensual being and cannot wait to taste life to its fullest. She leaves home at 18, goes to California to play semipro basketball. A flapper in the twenties, she goes on to own a restaurant and bar in San Francisco and marries at least four times.

LAVERNE (Younger).........[Act I] The baby of the family; she is 12 years old. Headstrong, at 16, she runs away and heads to Alaska to find her adventure in life. She goes on to write country western music.

LAVERNE (Adult)................[Act II] Twenty years later; now 32 years old and a raw boned pioneer woman who has been living in Alaska her entire adult life.

THE GUYER GIRLS

ACT I – SCENE I

(SETTING: Tumwater, Washington. 1920. The kitchen in a large farm house.)

(AT RISE: It is just dawn and SOPHIA GUYER (MAMA) is busy at the stove cooking breakfast. Stage left is a staircase leading upstairs.)

MAMA. *(Calling up the stairs.)* Girls! Breakfast is ready!

(MAMA turns back to the stove. VIOLET, 16 years old, is a budding beauty. SHE tumbles down the stairs and stands in the middle of the kitchen. VIOLET's hair is up in rags.)

VIOLET. Morning, Mama.
MAMA. *(Turning to greet VIOLET.)* Good morning, did you... *(MAMA's eyes grow huge with shock.)* My gracious, Violet, what happened to your eyebrows?

(VIOLET touches where her eyebrows should be and rushes to the mirror over the sink.)

VIOLET. *(Shrieks)* OH! That witch! That monster! She cut off my eyebrows! *(Leaning closer to the mirror.)* Oh no! Look at my eyelashes! Oh, Mama, look at me!
MAMA. I am looking, daughter. What on earth happened?
VIOLET. *(VIOLET begins to cry.)* The dance is only two weeks away. Oh, Mama, look at what Ivah has done!

MAMA. *(MAMA steps to the foot of the stairs.)* Ivah! Get down here! Now!

IVAH. *(Calls from offstage.)* Yes, Mama. *(IVAH walks slowly down the stairs. IVAH is seventeen and pretty in a tomboyish way.)* Yes, Mama?

MAMA. *(She takes VIOLET by the shoulders and turns her away from the mirror to face IVAH.)* Ivah, did you do this to your sister?

IVAH. Mama....

MAMA. Don't lie to me. You know that I know when you girls are lying. Answer me—did you do this?

IVAH. Yes, but Mama....

MAMA. Don't 'but Mama' me. What in the world? Why?

IVAH. *(IVAH holds up her hands, showing very short fingernails.)* She cut off all my beautiful fingernails, Mama....

VIOLET. You're always scratching me...

IVAH. I am not! You're just jealous because I have lovely hands and long fingernails...

VIOLET. Oh, hang your 'lovely hands'. Jimmy doesn't...

MAMA. Hush! Both of you! Always squabbling...what am I going to do with the two of you?

IVAH. *(Holding up her hands again.)* But, Mama., look...

MAMA. I said, be quiet. Ivah, what in the world is the matter with you? Last week it was the outhouses...don't you two dare laugh. It may seem that tipping over outhouses is a harmless prank to you but let us not forget that Mrs. Pruitt was in one of them at the time. It took both of her boys to haul her out of that hole.

(At the mention of the outhouses BOTH girls look at each other and then quickly away, trying not to laugh.)

IVAH. I told you, Mama, we didn't know Mrs. Pruitt was in there...

MAMA. Never mind that. Now this week you mutilate your sister.

VIOLET. I can't, I won't go to school looking like this. What am I going to do, Mama? I hate her! *(VIOLET turns to IVAH.)* I hate you!

MAMA. No, you don't hate your sister. They'll grow back. I can paint your eyebrows in until they do. Mascara should do the trick with your lashes. You can stay home today. I'll write your teacher a note which... *(Looking sternly at IVAH.)* ...Ivah will deliver this morning. And you, young lady, as part of your punishment you will bring Violet's lessons to her after school and help her with them.

IVAH. *(Whining.)* I can't...I'll lose my job. You know I have to get right to work after school.

MAMA. Yes, you can and you will. In the evenings, after school and work, you will help your sister with her lessons until she can return to school.

IVAH. But, Mama...

MAMA. No 'buts', Ivah. The alternative is I cut off your eyelashes and eyebrows. You decide.

IVAH. Yes, Ma'am.

MAMA. Now, tomorrow's Saturday. You will stay home and help me clean Lillas' room. She gets in on Monday.

IVAH. *(Indignant.)* But Patsy, Pam, and I go to the matinee every Saturday, Mama.

MAMA. All this mischief you get into has consequences. You have to learn that once and for all. You will stay home three Saturdays as the rest of your punishment.

IVAH. Mama! *(Trying a different tack.)* What about Vi? What's she going to do all day? She cut off my fingernails...what's her punishment?

MAMA. Oh, I think no eyebrows or lashes is plenty punishment for one girl. Now, you two finish setting the table. Violet, get your sister down here for breakfast.

VIOLET. *(Moving to the stairs, SHE yells up.)* Vernie, breakfast! Get up! You'll be late again.

MAMA. Violet! I could have yelled. Go up, like a lady, and get your sister.

VIOLET. Yes, Ma'am.

> *(As VIOLET starts up LAVERNE, a coltish, twelve year old comes down the stairs, with a great amount of clatter.)*

LAVERNE. 'Morning, Mama. 'Morning, Ivy. 'Morning... *(Gets a good look at VIOLET.)* Holy Christopher!

MAMA. LaVerne, watch your mouth. Ladies don't swear.

LAVERNE. That wasn't a swear word, Mama.... *(Amazed.)* Look at Vi...

MAMA. It came very close, young lady.

> *(Eyes like saucers, LAVERNE keeps talking. She is fascinated by gruesome diseases and events.)*

LAVERNE. Sorry, Mama. Vi, what happened to your face? Do you have some terrible disease? Is your hair going to fall out too? Are you going to die? Jeepers!

VIOLET. Don't be silly, Vernie...I am not dying. Your dumb sister did this...

LAVERNE. *(In no doubt as to which sister VIOLET refers.)* Ivy...

IVAH. What'd I tell you about the name, squirt? Don't call me Ivy! I am not a plant.

LAVERNE. But, Iv—ah, what'd you do that to Vi for? *(Giggles.)* She looks terrible.

IVAH. *(Shooting daggers at VIOLET, SHE holds her hands up for LAVERNE to inspect.)* Look at what she did to my nails.

LAVERNE. Holy...

(MAMA gives her a stern look.)

Jeepers! Your beautiful nails, Ivy...

MAMA. Sit down girls. Breakfast is ready.

(As the GIRLS sit down, MAMA moves around the large table dishing eggs onto everyone's plate.)

VIOLET. Where's Papa?

MAMA. Oh, he was up hours ago. Gone already. He wanted to get some trees down before the sawyers show up.

VIOLET. When will he be home?

MAMA. Probably Sunday. He thought that section would take them at least two days. Why?

VIOLET. Nothing. *(Beat.)* Lillas. wrote that she wanted to talk to you and Papa and asked me, did I know for sure if he would be home.

LAVERNE. *(Sing-song.)* Lilla's got a secret...Lilla's got a secret....

VIOLET. Shut up, Vernie! You don't know what you're talking about, as usual.

LAVERNE. Do too.

VIOLET. Do not.

MAMA. Girls, please, hush. Violet, do you know what Lillas wants to discuss with us?

VIOLET. No, Ma'am. She just asked. I wrote back that Papa was working the trees out by Olympia and I didn't know if he'd get home.

IVAH. How did she get time off from her job, Mama? How's she getting home?

MAMA. They gave her a couple of days off since work was slow. She's riding down from Seattle with the Porters. All right then. Ivah, LaVerne, you're going to be late for school. Hurry up now. Violet, you can help me clear up here.

(IVAH and LAVERNE gather their books and coats, kiss MAMA and exiting, THEY begin whispering and giggling.)

VIOLET. *(Yells after IVAH.)* We'll see how funny you think this is, Ivah Sue, when I exact my revenge…

(IVAH laughs even louder as she exits.)

MAMA. Whatever could Lillas want to tell us?
VIOLET. *(Sworn to secrecy.)* Don't know, Mama.

(As LIGHTS fade, VIOLET and MAMA are clearing the table.)

ACT I~SCENE 2

(AT RISE: MAMA and the YOUNGER GIRLS sit at the kitchen table with LILLAS. LILLAS is nineteen and beautiful. As lights come up they are all laughing. Cups of tea are on the table. A glass of milk sits in front of LAVERNE.)

LILLAS. *(To IVAH)* I declare Vi's eyebrows, or lack of, are going to rank right up there with your farts…What were you thinking, Ivah?
MAMA. Lillas! What language!
VIOLET. She's a beast!
IVAH. *(IVAH shrugs.)* She had it coming.

LaVERNE. That story's my very favorite. *(Yelling.)* Tell that one! Tell that one!

MAMA. Now see what you've started, Lillas. LaVerne, you are not to bring that up again. Ladies do not speak of such things.

(All the GIRLS look at each other and then break out in laughter, including MAMA.)

VIOLET. In honor of Lilla' being home, let me tell the story of the perfume bottle...please?

LaVERNE. *(Jumping up and down in her chair.)* Yes, please do, Mama.

IVAH. *(Droll.)* I don't know what all the fuss is about. Mrs. Pruitt loves perfume.

VIOLET. Let me tell...

LILLAS. Let her tell it, Mama. It's the best story.

MAMA. Oh, very well then—but, Violet, this is the very last time that story gets told in this house.

(EVERYONE looks at VIOLET and leans in, anticipating a well-told story. It doesn't matter that they have all heard it many times.)

VIOLET. Well, Mrs. Pruitt...

LaVERNE. No! No, start at the very beginning. You always start with how old I was and how old Ivah was...

VIOLET. Okay, squirt. You were seven years old and so Ivah was twelve. I was eleven. Lillas was fourteen...

LILLAS. And way too old for such shenanigans...

(VIOLET and IVAH both stick their tongues out at LILLAS.)

LaVERNE. Shhh...let Vi tell the story.

VIOLET. Anyway, Mrs. Pruitt was really mean. Hasn't changed much if you ask me.

MAMA. *(Can't stand Mrs. Pruitt either.)* Violet, be Christian. She's had a hard life.

VIOLET. Well, she didn't have to tell you about the streetcar rails. I call that pretty mean. She could've just minded her own business. Anyway, after our punishment for pulling up the streetcar rails, we got together—me and Ivah—and decided that Mrs. Pruitt needed a good lesson about tattling. So, we saved up our chore-money and when we got enough we went down to the five and dime and got the most beautiful, carved glass bottle we could buy. We bought ribbon to tie around the neck and made a card out of some of Mama's good paper. Then we waited for one of Mama's ham hock and bean dinners. The day after the beans, Ivah and I went out back into the woods and Ivah broke wind into that little fancy bottle.

LaVERNE. Ivah's got the best farts ever!

MAMA. Vernie!

IVAH. I do not!

VIOLET. Do too.

LaVERNE. Uh–huh.

VIOLET. *(To IVAH.)* Well, you had some pretty foul wind that day, let me tell you. *(Beat.)* Anyway, Ivah filled the bottle good and we stopped 'er up. We tied the fancy ribbon around the neck and wrote on the card, 'from a secret admirer'. That night we snuck over to Mrs. Pruitt's front porch and left it by the door. The next morning, we hid in her bushes to watch for her. She comes sashaying out the front door looking for her newspaper. She's got her old ratty chenille bathrobe on and her hair is up in rags. She spots the fancy perfume bottle, picks it up and reads the card. If she'd had feathers she would have puffed up like a peacock. She stands right there and pulls the cork out of the bottle and takes a big whiff—

MAMA. Oh, my stars...

VIOLET. *(Gleefully.)* Then she gives this funny little scream, drops the bottle and faints dead away. *(Laughing.)* Oh, my! It was the funniest thing I ever saw. Ivah wet her pants, she was laughing so hard.

IVAH. I did not.

VIOLET. Did so.

LaVERNE. Did you get caught?

VIOLET. No, and we didn't tell Mama for years after. Mrs. Pruitt came over and tried to tell Mama that we had done it, but Mama said she couldn't punish her girls unless Mrs. Pruitt had proof.

MAMA. By the time you girls told me I couldn't, for the life of me, think of an appropriate punishment. And, I wasn't about to tell Mrs. Pruitt that my girls had done such a vile thing.

IVAH. The old witch deserved it. She thinks she's so much better than everyone else...

MAMA. Ivah...

LaVERNE. Now, tell the one about the seals and the Victrola, Lillas.

LILLAS. Mama?

MAMA. All right. But that's the last story tonight, LaVerne. You are well past your bedtime as it is.

LILLAS. When you were just a baby, Vernie, Ivah and I would take Vi out in a rowboat that Papa had when we lived in Olympia. When Mama wasn't looking, we would take her Victrola with us.

LaVERNE. *(Jumping up and down, SHE knows the answer before she asks.)* Why? Why, Lilla'? What did you need music for?

LILLAS. Well, Pumpkin, in the late spring—if you catch it just right—you can row out into the Sound for a special treat. Vi and Ivah would take turns cranking the Victrola and I would row, 'cause I'm the strongest. We always played some happy, jumpy song. Can you guess why?

LaVERNE. I know, I know! The dolphins!

LILLAS. That's right. We'd row around for a bit, cranking on that old Victrola and pretty soon here they'd come. Six or eight dolphins playing

and splashin' and following the music. Then we got the bright idea to take some smelt out with us to feed them. That's why they were there in the Sound; for the smelt runs. Well, we'd have a regular party for those guys.
LAVERNE. Would they follow you forever?
LILLAS. As long as the music and the food lasted.

(VIOLET, IVAH, and LILLAS all laugh at the memory.)

IVAH. Of course, we would have to sneak the record player back into the house before Mama caught us.
MAMA. It took me two summers to figure out why my Victrola had rust on it. Do you girls remember the whippin' you got?
VIOLET. *(All the GIRLS shudder)* We sure do, Mama. But, what hurt most was us having to go out and cut the switches *(Laughing)* you were going to use on us.
MAMA. You deserved a whippin'! It's a wonder that heavy old Victrola didn't sink the boat with you three hellions in it!
VIOLET. *(SHE jumps up and runs around the table to hug MAMA.)* Mama, those whippings never hurt much, you know. We'd always cut a real small switch.
MAMA. And you think I didn't know that? Now, off you go—the bunch of you. Your sister and I have some serious conversing to do.
LAVERNE. Oh, Mama, do we have to?
IVAH. Yeah, how come we can't stay and talk too?
VIOLET. How come Lillas gets to stay up late and we don't?
MAMA. Because I say so. No more sass. Go on, get to bed. We'll see you all in the morning.

(The three GIRLS reluctantly troop up the stairs. MAMA gets up and pours hot water into the tea pot.)

MAMA. I declare, these girls are going to be the death of me. You were never so difficult. When I first saw Violet's eyebrows...

LILLAS. *(Laughing.)* Oh, Mama, Vi and Ivah will never change. You might as well give up and let them have at it.

MAMA. What did you want to speak to your father and me about, Lillas?

LILLAS. I wish Papa could be here...it's important and I wanted to tell you together.

MAMA. He's disappointed too, dear. But, that storm set their work back and the time on the license to cut is running out. He'll see you next time. *(Looking at LILLAS hard.)* What's so important that your father has to be here?

LILLAS. I don't know how to tell you, Mama.... I know you had big plans for me, and...

MAMA. Just spit it out, girl. You know you'll feel better if you do.

LILLAS. Remember I wrote you about a young man I was seeing—Richard?

MAMA. Yes, I do. Didn't you say he was with the Consulate's office or something?

LILLAS. Uh-huh. He's on the staff involved in the stabilization of Europe now that the war is over. I'm not completely sure what his job is. But, he left last week for London and he'll be gone at least six months.

MAMA. Oh, I'm sorry, Lillas. *(Beat. Then MAMA brightens.)* But, there are other nice young men out there. You'll see, you'll meet someone else.

LILLAS. No I won't, Mama.

MAMA. Of course you will...you're young and beautiful...

LILLAS. I'm in love with Richard.

MAMA. Oh pish, Lillas. You'll fall in love dozens of times and...

LILLAS. *(Cutting her off.)* Richard and I got married before he left.

MAMA. What! What do you mean, you got married? Without your family? You wouldn't!

LILLAS. I did. There was no time for planning or family. I wanted you and Papa and the girls there but it was such a rush. We didn't have time to plan anything. He left the next day.

MAMA. Lillas Elizabeth Guyer! What were you thinking? It could have waited until he came back.

LILLAS. No, it couldn't, Mama.

MAMA. Six months is nothing. We could have spent the time planning the wedding.

LILLAS. No, Mama. We couldn't wait six months...

MAMA. My word, you children are always in such a hurry. I can't imagine what was in your head, Lillas—to get married, all alone with no family around you.... What must his family think?

(LILLAS doesn't know how to tell her mother, so she blurts out the real news.)

LILLAS. I'M GOING TO HAVE A BABY! *(SHE begins to cry.)* We had to get married before he left. Oh, Mama, I love him so much and now he's gone...

MAMA. *(Rises and goes to LILLAS. SHE wraps her daughter in her arms.)* Oh, Lilla', my little girl. Why didn't you send for me? A baby...why, I don't know what to say.

(Just then VIOLET, IVAH, and LAVERNE tumble down the stairs, screaming and laughing. They have been listening at the top of the stairs. They all gather around LILLAS and EVERYONE is talking all at once.)

VIOLET. Oh, Lilla', you're married!	**IVAH.** A baby! We're going to have a baby!

LaVERNE. Who? Who's having a baby?

VIOLET. *[To LaVERNE.]* Lillas is.

MAMA. What are you girls doing down here?

IVAH. When? What do you want, Lilla', a boy or a girl?

MAMA. Girls, girls, hush! Why aren't you in bed?

IVAH. Mama, please, please let us stay. We want to hear about Richard and the baby.

LaVERNE. Who's Richard? What baby?!

MAMA. *(Exchanging looks with LILLAS.)* All right, you can stay. You girls have been through every thing else together no need to change that now. Go ahead, Lillas, this story is yours to tell.

VIOLET. Start at the very beginning.

LILLAS. I met Richard last year. He's been courting me all this time.

LaVERNE. *(Sighing.)* How did you and Richard meet? Was it a star-filled night?

LILLAS. *(Grinning at LaVERNE.)* Yes, it was at night and yes, there were stars out. The company I work for gave a dinner dance and Richard was invited. He's friends with my boss's son. That was how we were introduced.

LaVERNE. Then what? Don't leave anything out.

LILLAS. Richard asked me to dance that very first dance. He kept coming back and asking me to dance again... *(sighs)* ...and again. He told me later that he fell in love with me that night.

IVAH. Yuk!

VIOLET. Did he walk you home?

MAMA. That's wouldn't have been proper, Violet *(Turns to LILLAS.)* Did he? Walk you home?

LILLAS. No, Mama. I *did* remember some of what you taught me.

MAMA. *(Sardonically.)* Apparently, not quite enough.

LAVERNE. *(Confused by all the adult talk and innuendos.)* Whaddya mean, Mama? What was Lilla' suppose to remember?

MAMA. Never mind, Vernie. Finish please, Lillas. We're going to be here all night.

LILLAS. The next day he sent me flowers at work with a note saying he would like to see me again.

VIOLET. Oh! Flowers! What kind? How big was the bouquet?

MAMA. Good grief! We're going to be here 'til next week. Girls, let her tell and stop interrupting.

LILLAS. Daisies. A big bunch of them. Anyway, we started seeing one another; at first with another couple and in groups of friends.

IVAH. Weren't you ever alone?

MAMA. *(Pointedly.)* Evidently they were at some point.

LILLAS. *(Ignoring MAMA.)* So then about a month ago, Richard was told that he was being transferred to London for six months. He wanted to take me with him but wives and girl friends are not allowed. It's too soon after the war.

VIOLET. So you got married. *(Sighs.)* How romantic.

LILLAS. Yes. Richard asked me to marry him before he left.

LAVERNE. And now there's a baby?

LILLAS. Yes, Vernie, now there's a baby.

LAVERNE. *(Eyes round with amazement, SHE turns to MAMA.)* You were right, Mama! You *do* have to be married to get a baby!

> *(EVERYONE bursts into laughter. LILLAS hugs her baby sister.)*

ACT I~SCENE 3

(AT RISE: LILLAS sits with MAMA at the kitchen table. Her coat is draped over the back of a chair. LILLAS has a hat on, and a small suitcase sits on the floor. They are having a final cup of tea before Lillas leaves to go back to Seattle.)

MAMA. I don't see why you can't live here while Richard's gone, dear girl. We've plenty of room, for you and the baby.

LILLAS. Mama, I told you. I have a job, I have an apartment with roommates that are relying on me for rent. Besides, I want to be exactly where Richard left me so he can find me.

MAMA. Couldn't you write to him...let him know you moved home?

LILLAS. I promise I'll come home when my time is near if Richard hasn't come back. *(Unsure of the future.)* But, he promised to be here with me, when the baby comes.

MAMA. My head's in a whirl. I can't believe this is happening to you. Of all my girls, you were always the sensible one. It's Ivah I always thought I had to keep a tighter rein on...but you...

LILLAS. I know, Mama. I'm sorry.

MAMA. No, no, don't be sorry. It's not the end of the world. You're in love and thank God, you're married. It's just that you're so young...

LILLAS. Mama, you were barely fifteen when you had your first baby. I'm nineteen. Practically an old maid.

MAMA. I know...but I wanted better for you. Married with a baby coming...it's harder than you will ever know.

LILLAS. What do you mean? I've married the man I love with all my heart and now we're going to have a baby—one we made out of our love. How can you say that's going to be hard?

MAMA. Oh, child, you are so innocent. And I guess that's as it should be. When I met your father I was young but so much wiser...

LILLAS. Tell that story, Mama, we have time and it's, as Vernie would say, my all time favorite. *(Beat.)* But, Mama, I'm a married woman now. Tell me the whole story about you and Papa.

MAMA. What ever do you mean?

LILLAS. I always had the feeling that you left the best parts out. You did, didn't you?

(MAMA examines LILLAS' face and resigned, begins the story.)

MAMA. It was 1893. Your father, Levi Guya, lived in Paris. I was fourteen and lived on a small farm outside the city. My father had his own bit of land but we worked for the Duc of Caumont. They owned the Chalet and all the land for as far as you could see. *(MAMA gazes far off, remembering.)* There was a son, Stephan, sixteen and very handsome. He paid me attention. One day he caught me in the dairy barn, alone, and kissed me. He kept telling me, 'Sophia, you are the most beautiful girl in the village, in the Province, in the world. I love you!' He kept kissing me and then I was kissing him back. One thing led to another and before I knew it, things were going too far. I told him, 'No' and to stop but he wouldn't listen.

LILLAS. Oh, Mama...he raped you?

MAMA. They call it that now. But, in those days it was being 'forced'.

LILLAS. What happened?

MAMA. If it was the Duke's son, you didn't complain or tell. Who were you going to tell anyway? Your father and mother worked for the Caumont family and no one else would have cared.

MAMA. They would have smirked at the boy who was sowing his oats and treated me like a whore. The only thing for me to do, was to hope that there would be no baby.

LILLAS. *(Realization hits her.)* Poor Mama! The baby...was Jerry?

MAMA. Yes. Jeremiah Peter. I told Stephan about the baby, thinking that he loved me. He laughed at me. He called me names. I never saw him again.

LILLAS. But, how did Papa...?

MAMA. Shortly after that I realized that I was pregnant. One day my father took me to market to help with the stall and the milk and eggs. Your Papa was there with his family.

MAMA. He stayed by our stall the whole day. Well, let me tell you, after my experience in the barn, I wanted nothing to do with any other young man. I completely ignored him...I was even rude.

LILLAS. *(Laughing.)* You? Rude? Never!

MAMA. Levi would not give up no matter how I acted toward him...he brought me a cold drink, he brought me a wild flower, he bought me some earrings which my father immediately returned to him with a harsh scolding. Before the day was over, Levi's father came to my father and asked if they could 'have our direction' and Father's permission for Levi 'to call'. My father was stunned by such formality and respect. A family from Paris, of all things, interested in a daughter of his.

LILLAS. What happened? Well, I know what happened, we're all here for heaven's sake but...Mama... *(In a hushed tone.)* ...you were pregnant and alone. Did you tell?

MAMA. No, I couldn't. So, my father allowed Levi to come to call. I cried and pleaded with him, told him I didn't even like Levi, which wasn't true. My father said I was not going to throw away a chance like that without even getting to know the young man. So, Levi came. He was so nice and respectful. He and I would walk out. That's what they called it then. But he would always make sure that we could be seen from the house. *(MAMA smiles with her memories.)* I wasn't very nice to him in the beginning. Sometimes I wouldn't even see him. I would fake a headache or some other nonsense. My father was furious with me. But, your dear sweet Papa just kept coming back. I guess he wore me down. Then one day we were walking through the fields and we came to a lovely patch of wild flowers. Well, he knelt down in those flowers and asked me to marry him.

LILLAS. Oh, Mama!

MAMA. I was three months along by then. I burst out crying. Sobbing really. I had grown very fond of your Papa and knew he would run away when I told him the truth.

LILLAS. You told him right then, didn't you?

(MAMA nods.)

What did he say?

MAMA. I was crying so hard, I couldn't talk. He stood up and took me into his arms. I will never forget how safe I felt in those moments. Then when I had stopped my blubbering, for the most part, he handed me his handkerchief and asked me if I liked him even a little bit. That started the water works all over again. I blurted out that I liked him more than a little. He stepped away and took both of my hands into his and told me no matter what it was, I could tell him and we would solve it together.

LILLAS. *(Sighing.)* Oh, Mama.

MAMA. Yes, it was the most romantic thing ever. But, that's your Papa to this very day.

LILLAS. What did you say? How did you explain?

MAMA. I told him the truth…the entire story.

LILLAS. Oh! Weren't you frightened? What did Papa do?

MAMA. At first, he wanted to kill Stephan. *(Laughing.)* Oh, you should have seen him, he was so fierce.

LILLAS. My sweet, gentle Papa—fierce?

MAMA. Oh yes, he was quite the passionate man. *(Beat.)* Anyway, he said he didn't care that the baby wasn't his. He said he would love it as his very own. Said we must be married immediately. The banns were read that next Sunday and we were married three weeks later.

LILLAS. Then what? Was that when you and Papa lived in Paris?

MAMA. Yes, until Jerry was born, we lived with his parents. That didn't work out very well. *(Sardonically.)* You see, his mother could count. She never forgave me that the child was someone else's.

LILLAS. *(Knows a good deal of the story already.)* And that's when your and Papa's 'big adventure' began. You sailed for America.

MAMA. Yes. We landed on Ellis Island. Jerry was only two months old. We thought the streets of New York would be paved in gold. Oh, but, you know the story...

LILLAS. Oh, no, Mama, go on. I love this part.

MAMA. I don't want you to miss your train, dear.

LILLAS. I've got hours yet. Please finish the story. *(Taking up the tale from where MAMA had left off.)* You changed our name from 'Guya' to 'Guyer' because Papa said it sounded more American.

MAMA. No one could pronounce 'Guy-yeah' correctly. When we arrived in New York, we had been given some people's names who would help us—so your Papa and I went to the Bowery to find them. They took us in for a time until we could find our own place...

LILLAS. *(LILLAS picks up the story.)* It was just one room with a shared bathroom down the hall. It was called a 'cold water flat', and Papa hated it.

MAMA. Yes. Jerry was sickly. It seemed like we were never warm enough. One day Papa came home from the docks and said, 'Enough! I didn't come all this way to have my family live like this—in dirt and noise and poverty'. He had heard that there were jobs 'out west' and he talked to some men that were going to some place called Seattle...to work in the woods.

LILLAS. *(Resuming the story again.)* And so you and Papa and little Jerry headed west. Oh, Mama, you were so brave...

MAMA. Not brave. We didn't know any better. Papa just knew that he didn't want any more cities. We took a train as far as St. Louis and caught the flat boat that traveled the Missouri river between St. Louis and Great Falls, Montana.

LILLAS. And you survived rapids and snowstorms and bears and Indians.

MAMA. Peaceful Indians, small rapids, and placid bears, thank God.

LILLAS. And in Montana you joined a group going on to Seattle, right?

MAMA. You can tell this story better than I can, child.

LILLAS. Oh, no, Mama. Go on, tell the end.

MAMA. So we traveled by train, boat and wagon to Seattle. I'll never forget the trip up the Missouri River. It seemed like every other day we would get stuck on a sandbar and have to be pulled off. The Indians would come out to the boat to trade. They were half-naked and all painted up. But, the guides told us that their warpaint was adornment, like a woman wearing jewelry. They scared me half to death. All we mothers were so certain that they would steal our babies. Then we crossed the mountains in wagons and finally arrived in Seattle. Now, Seattle wasn't as big as Paris or New York, but it was as dirty and rough with a saloon on every corner. The jobs in the woods were south so your Papa tucked your brother and I up in a hotel room while he came down to Tumwater to see about a job. And that's where we've been ever since, raising our ten children and living our life. *(Beat.)* Oh, my, look at the time. We'd better get you down to the train.

(THEY both rise. LILLAS crosses to MAMA and hugs her.)

LILLAS. It's going to be all right, Mama. Richard loves me and you'll see, everything will turn out just fine. I promise.

ACT I~SCENE 4

(AT RISE: Two years later. The kitchen. Mama is at the stove cooking breakfast. Violet, now eighteen, is coming down the stairs.)

VIOLET. 'Morning, Mama..

MAMA. 'Morning, child. Get your sisters, will you? Breakfast is just about ready.

(VIOLET. turns on the stairs and yells.)

VIOLET. Ivah! Vernie! Breakfast!

MAMA. Good Lord, Vi, do you have to yell?

VIOLET. *(Petulant.)* Why am I always the one that has to go get them? Do they always have to be late?

MAMA. *(Whirls around.)* Well, aren't we a "sassy-pants" this morning. Is that how you speak to me?

VIOLET. Sorry, Mama.

MAMA. What's wrong, child?

VIOLET. I don't know… *(Beat.)* The dance…why did Ivah get asked and I didn't? I'm way prettier than she is.

MAMA. I've told you before, Violet, 'pretty is as pretty does'.

VIOLET. *(Begins setting the table.)* I know you keep saying that, but you never told me exactly what it means.

MAMA. It means that sometimes your actions are not very 'pretty'. A real lady is pleasant to be around, agreeable, with nice manners. *(Beat.)* Yes, you're pretty, but it's not nice to act like you know you're pretty. And really, Violet, your mouth is frequently open and talking before your good sense kicks in. You're far too impulsive.

VIOLET. Oh, pish, Mama, I just speak the truth. People are so phony—I can't stand most of them.

VIOLET. And the other girls are so prissy and helpless when the boys are around. When the truth is, some of them could lift a mule.

MAMA. *(Laughing.)* I know, but that is just the kind of observation that keeps you from getting asked to the dances.

VIOLET. *(Throwing herself into a chair.)* I don't care. They're just a bunch of babies. Someday I am going to meet a real man and he will respect me for my brain.

MAMA. *(Dryly.)* I sincerely hope so.

(LAVERNE, now 14, rattles down the stairs. She is homely in a cute way and caught between being a child and being a woman. SHE rushes up to MAMA and gives her a noisy kiss.)

LAVERNE. Good Morning, Mama! Can I have pancakes? And your blackberry syrup? Please?

MAMA. School morning, LaVerne. No time for pancakes. Maybe Saturday you might find them on the menu.

LAVERNE. Oh, Mama., can we have menus. *(Beat.)* We could, Mama. I could write them for you.

MAMA. Maybe next week. Now get the milk and sit. Where's your sister?

(Just then, IVAH walks slowly down the stairs. SHE is very subdued and quiet. SHE sits in a chair, despondent.)

MAMA. Who wants tea? Ivah?

IVAH. No thanks, Mama, I'm not hungry.

VIOLET. *(Sarcastic.)* That's a switch!

IVAH. Shut up, you little twit!

VIOLET. You shut up!

IVAH. No, you!

MAMA. Girls! For heaven's sake, stop bickering. Ivah, you'll need something. If not breakfast, at least have a cup of tea and some toast.

IVAH. *(Folds her arms on the table and puts her head on her arms.)* No! I couldn't bear to eat anything!

VIOLET. Oh, brother! What now?

MAMA. Violet, hush! That's exactly what I was talking about before.

VIOLET. *(Whining.)* What?

MAMA. The 'pretty is as pretty does'?

VIOLET. *(Confused.)* But, Mama, it's Ivah. Surely, that doesn't apply to sisters.

MAMA. Yes, dear, I'm afraid that it does. *(Beat.)* Ivah, dear, what's the matter? Didn't you sleep well?

LAVERNE. I bet it was the dance, Mama. What's wrong, Ivy, were you a wallflower?

IVAH. *(IVAH. raises her head.)* Mama., make them leave me alone. *(SHE puts her head back down.)*

MAMA. Girls, leave your sister alone. Ivah, we can't help if you don't spit it out…you'll feel better if you do.

IVAH. *(Raising her head, her eyes are full of tears.)* I met the man of my dreams last night.

MAMA. And that's making you cry?

VIOLET. She's always meeting the 'man of her dreams'.

LAVERNE. What's he look like, Ivy?

VIOLET. He's probably married.

IVAH. Shut up, Vi! You don't know anything!

MAMA. What happened, child?

IVAH. *(Ignoring her sisters.)* His name is Arthur…Arthur Gibbons. He's a junior partner at a law firm in Seattle. He's just wonderful, Mama..

MAMA. I'm sure he is.

IVAH. Billy Murphy introduced us.

LAVERNE. *(Never getting an answer.)* What's he look like, Ivy? *(Sighing dramatically.)* You're always getting ahead of the story.
IVAH. Oh, he's wonderful! Tall, with sandy brown hair and the most beautiful eyes—sort of hazel.
IVAH. He was wearing the most beautiful suit I have ever seen; the material was so soft.
VIOLET. I think I'm going to puke.
LAVERNE. Oooo...he sounds divine...
IVAH. Mama, make her shut up!
MAMA. Violet, be quiet.
IVAH. There was a waltz and he asked me to dance. He complimented me on my dress. He said I should always wear blue. I asked him why and he said it brought out the blue of my eyes.
VIOLET. Now I know I'm going to puke!
LAVERNE. I'm going to swoon!
MAMA. *(Ignoring them.)* Go on, dear. He's sounds the perfect gentleman. What happened to upset you?
IVAH. *(Indicating her two sisters.)* Oh, Mama, do I have to say in front of these two?
VIOLET. Sure do.
LAVERNE. Uh-huh.
IVAH. Mama!
MAMA. Girls, be quiet or you will go to your room. Go on, Ivah. It can't be that bad.
IVAH. *(Wailing.)* Yes, it is! You don't know... *(Beat.)* We were waltzing and suddenly I felt something brushing around my ankles. I stopped and looked down, and... *(SHE begins to cry.)* It was my drawers, Mama. The elastic broke and they were around my ankles...

(Pandemonium breaks out.)

VIOLET. *(Laughing.)* What! Your drawers fell down!

LAVERNE. Holy Christopher! **MAMA.** Oh, my!

LAVERNE. What'd you do, Ivy? Did you just die on the spot?

VIOLET. *(Laughing hysterically.)* Your drawers were down around your ankles? What'd Prince Charming do?

LAVERNE. Ran away, I bet.

MAMA. Girls! Hush! If I have to tell you again, you are no longer a part of this conversation. *(Turns back to IVAH.)* What did you do, dear?

IVAH. I looked up at Arthur. He was looking down at my ankles. Then he looked at me. Then he bent down, scooped up my drawers, and put them in his pocket. Took me back into his arms and continued the waltz.

MAMA. Oh, my.

IVAH. I couldn't bear to look at him. During the rest of the dance I stared at his shoulder. At the end of the dance, he escorted me to the Ladies' room and then calmly handed me my drawers. I mumbled something to him and ran into the Ladies'. I hid in there until the end of the night and everyone was gone. Oh, Mama, what am I going to do? Even if he wanted to see me again...

VIOLET. No worry about that.

IVAH. You shut up!

MAMA. *(Warning her.)* Violet.

VIOLET. I'm just saying...

IVAH. Even if he did...I could never face him again, not ever!

MAMA. I'm sure it's not that bad.

VIOLET. Oh yes it is.

LAVERNE. I would just die!

MAMA. Think on the good side, Ivah. What a gentleman, to rescue you like that. If he's all you say he is, he will want to see you again.

VIOLET. If for no other reason, to see if you have drawers that'll stay up!

(IVAH jumps out of her chair, bent on physically injuring VIOLET. VIOLET jumps behind MAMA's chair, laughing.)

IVAH. I'm going to kill you!
MAMA. *(Holding Ivah by the arm.)* Violet! Go to your room immediately!
VIOLET. Ma—ma!
MAMA. If you can't support you sister, go! Ivah, sit down.

(Glaring at VIOLET, IVAH sits back down. VIOLET runs up the stairs. The telephone rings off stage.)

LaVERNE. *(Jumping up, SHE runs off stage left.)* I'll get it!
IVAH. Oh Mama, it was just awful...
MAMA. I know, dear.

(Almost immediately, LAVERNE runs back on. Her eyes are huge.)

MAMA. Who was it?
LaVERNE. It's for you, Ivy. *(SHE whispers.)* I think it's HIM!
IVAH. Oh, no. Mama, I can't talk to him, I can't!
MAMA. You certainly can. Just pretend nothing happened. I'm sure that's what he will do.
LaVERNE. Hurry up, Ivy, he's waiting. What if he hangs up?

(At those words, IVAH runs off stage left. MAMA. starts clearing the table.)

MAMA. LaVerne, go on upstairs and finish getting ready for school.
LaVERNE. But Mama, I want to hear what happens.
MAMA. You'll hear what happens after school. Go on now.
LaVERNE. Jeepers. I always miss the good parts.

(LaVERNE slowly tramps up the stairs. As SHE exits, IVAH enters and crosses to the table. SHE sinks into a chair.)

MAMA. Well?
IVAH. *(Starry eyed.)* It was him, Mama. It was Arthur. You were right. He acted like nothing had happened.
MAMA. There, see, didn't I say? Why did he call?

(Looks up at MAMA, glowing with happiness.)

IVAH. He wants to take me boating, Sunday, on Green Lake. He says he will drive down so you and Papa can meet him and then we'll drive up to Seattle for the day. Oh, Mama.!
MAMA. *(Crossing to her daughter, she kisses her forehead.)* That's wonderful, child. See? Didn't I tell you? A real gentleman. *(Beat.)* Oh, goodness, look at the time. You'll be late if you don't hurry.

(IVAH. rises and races up the stairs. With doors banging, laughter and screaming can be heard upstairs. MAMA exits stage left.)

ACT I~SCENE 5

(AT RISE: MAMA sits at the kitchen table with her tea and is reading a letter. VIOLET comes on from stage left.)

VIOLET. Oh, has the mail come? Anything for me?

MAMA. Yes, you got a letter. It's there by your plate. Something from Oakland, California. *(Puzzled.)* We don't know anyone there. Probably an advertisement.

(VIOLET rushes over and sits at her place, grabs the letter and tears it open while talking.)

VIOLET. What are you reading, Mama?

MAMA. It's a letter from Lillas. *(Looks up smiling.)* They're coming home. Richard has been reassigned to the Seattle office.

VIOLET. That's wonderful! When are they coming? How's the baby?

MAMA. They are booked on a ship in... (Looks at the date on the letter and then glances at the calendar on the back wall.) ...two weeks. The baby's fine. Lillas says, *(MAMA reads from LILLAS' letter.)*

'Phyllis is growing like a little weed...all finished with teething and is sleeping like the proverbial baby. Can't wait for you to see your granddaughter, Mama—you won't believe how she has grown. This reassignment means a promotion for Richard. We're all looking forward to being home again. Tell the brats 'hello' for me. Love, your daughter, Lillas.'

VIOLET. How long does the crossing take, Mama?

MAMA. I think another two weeks, so they should be home in about a month.

(VIOLET goes back to her letter. As she reads, SHE gasps.)

MAMA. What's wrong? Who's that from?

VIOLET. Nothing...nothing's wrong. I just didn't expect... I didn't expect to get an answer this quickly.

MAMA. What answer? Who do we know in Oakland? *(MAMA reaches for the letter. VIOLET avoids her and stuffs the letter back into the envelope.)* Whatever is the matter with you?

VIOLET. *(Very serious.)* Mama, I want you to promise me you'll hear me out. Don't make any decisions until you hear me. Will you promise?

MAMA. What in the world is in that letter, Violet?

VIOLET. All my basketball playing in school has paid off. There's a semi-pro basketball league in San Francisco. They put an advertisement in the Seattle Times. *(Beat.)* I answered it.

MAMA. What!? Without telling me?

VIOLET. *(All in a rush, SHE is anxious to get it out before MAMA can say no.)* I never expected to hear from them, much less this quickly. I sent them sort of a resume of my basketball playing and a list of my letters and awards and how the team did. Well, they've answered and they want me to come down and play and let them take a look at me. All expenses paid.

MAMA. They want you to play basketball with a bunch of men?

VIOLET. *(Laughing.)* No, silly! It's a women's team.

MAMA. Well I never!

VIOLET. *(Grinning.)* I guess they were impressed with our team going to state. Imagine, Mama, <u>me</u> playing pro-basketball! *(Beat.)* Anyway, they want to see me. Please say I can go, Mama.

MAMA But, you're only eighteen, child. You're far too young to go off on your own. What were you thinking answering that advertisement.

VIOLET. *(Immediately ready to do battle.)* I'm not too young! Lillas. was nineteen and she got pregnant and had to get married. All I want to do is play basketball. You should feel lucky!

(MAMA is shocked that VIOLET knows this about LILLAS.)

MAMA. Violet! You are not to sass me! *(Beat.)* How do you know about Lillas.?

VIOLET. She told me. But, that doesn't matter. What matters is this chance to play semi-pro ball, Mama. Please, please let me go.

MAMA. I don't know what to think. I will have to talk it over with Papa.

(MAMA. has tears in her eyes. Just then, LAVERNE. comes down the stairs. SHE takes one look at MAMA. and knows something is terribly wrong.)

LAVERNE. Mama, what's wrong? You're crying!

MAMA. No, I'm not. I just got something in my eye.

VIOLET. Mama, don't cry. This is a wonderful thing that's happened.

LAVERNE. What? What's a wonderful thing? What's she talking about, Mama? Why are you crying?

VIOLET. I got a letter asking me to come play basketball in California, squirt.

(LAVERNE. takes one look at MAMA's tear streaked face and begins to howl.)

LAVERNE. No! I don't want you to go away! *(LAVERNE. throws herself at VIOLET.)* Everybody is going away! I don't want you to leave too. I'll be all alone.

(MAMA moves to LAVERNE and takes her into her arms. LAVERNE is crying like her heart will break.)

LAVERNE. I don't want Vi to go away. Tell her she can't Mama.
VIOLET. Vernie, don't cry. It's just a trip...I'll be back.
LAVERNE. No, it's not. You won't come back. You're leaving like everybody else.

(SHE continues to sob as MAMA holds her.)

VIOLET. Jeepers! Can't I do anything? I'm going and that's final!

(VIOLET rushes up the stairs. A door bangs shut.)

(Raising her head, LAVERNE looks at her mother. MAMA wipes the tears away.)

LAVERNE. What's wrong, Mama? Why is everyone leaving? Did I do something bad?
MAMA. Oh, sweetheart, of course you didn't. This is just how life is. People grow up and they move away. Someday, you'll grow up and go away.
LAVERNE. No I won't. I won't ever leave you, Mama.

INTERMISSION

ACT II~SCENE 1

(AT RISE: Twenty years later. Summer, 1941. MAMA sits at the kitchen table with LILLAS. They BOTH have letters in their hands. The tea pot and cups are inevitably present.)

MAMA. *(Waving a letter in the air.)* I received this letter from your sister, last week. Phillip's gone again.

LILLAS. Oh, dear. What happened? Vi threw him out...again?

MAMA. I really dislike that nick name, Lillas... I gave you girls the prettiest names I could find and you girls shorten everything! Really! "Vi" instead of "Violet". It's so...abrupt.

LILLAS. *(Laughing.)* Oh, Mama, you can be so Victorian at times. It's the forties—language changes, everything's faster. At home, my friends call me "Lil". Women are modern. It only took me four hours to get down here from Seattle...and I drove myself.

MAMA. *(Sighs.)* I guess you're right. I need to get with the times. *(Beat. Laughs.)* Anyway, back to "Vi".... She writes that Phillip will not stop gambling. She was afraid he'd gamble away the restaurant.

LILLAS. She would never let anything come between her and her restaurant...much less some man. She's a shrewd business woman.

MAMA. I'm still amazed at how well all my girls turned out. But, Phillip is the father of her children, for heaven's sake.

LILLAS. How will she manage with two little ones and no husband? I can't imagine my life without Richard.

MAMA. She says she has hired a girl to keep house and watch the kids while she runs the bar. In the slow times, she's taking in sewing and mending. Imagine! Mending for a bunch of women in the red light district. Whores!

LILLAS. Mama! *(Teasing her.)* Such language! You shock me.

MAMA. *(Embarrassed at herself.)* Well! That's what they are—and one of my daughters is associating with them! That's the kind of "modern woman" I can do without, thank you very much. *(Beat. Shaking her head, SHE reads more of the letter to herself.)* She says not to worry... Like I won't worry!

LILLAS. You know Vi, she always lands on her feet. She'll be okay, Mama.

MAMA. Not much I can do about it with me here and Violet in San Francisco. I do so dislike the idea of Violet working day and night and someone else raising my gran-babies. *(Sighs.)* What's Ivah got to say?

LILLAS. She wants to know when I'm coming back to Seattle. She goes on about what devilment we two could get into. *(Laughs.)* It makes no difference that she is married to a prominent lawyer, she will never change. Listen to this... *(LILLAS reads from the letter.)*

'...just the other day, Arthur came home just as I was coming in from a day digging in the garden. I was in my shorts and covered with dirt. Arthur said an important client was dropping by with some papers, so I said I would just hide in the kitchen and prepare dinner. About half an hour later, I heard the doorbell and then a little while later, I heard the front door close. Well! I'd heard so much about this particular client, I just had to get a look at him. So...hang on to your hat, sister dear, I got down on my hands and knees and crawled to the front dining room window so I could get a good look. Meanwhile, the important client was sitting on the sofa in the parlor, watching me sneak across the floor. I turned around and there he was, sitting there grinning at me. It turns out that it was the paperboy who had come to the door to collect and the client hadn't left at all.'

MAMA. Oh, my.

LILLAS. Yes, indeed... *(SHE reads on.)* Well, we all had a good laugh and the client stayed for dinner.

MAMA. Arthur is a patient man.

LILLAS. He is that, but I think that's why he married Ivah. She's wild and interesting and he will never be bored with her. *(Beat.)* Any word from Vernie, Mama?

*(This is a tender subject for **MAMA**, as **LAVERNE**, has been gone for many years after running away to Alaska.)*

MAMA. LaVerne called the other day. She's still writing her music and sending it out. She was in good spirits and was kidding about her stacks and stacks of rejection letters from music companies. She's met a logger up there in Fairbanks. I think she said his name was Milo. She thought it would make me happy to know she was with a woodsman like Papa.

LILLAS. Do you think she will ever come home?

MAMA. I don't know, child. I don't feel as if I know her at all. She was such a little homebody when she was young. Then, one day, to walk into her bedroom and find that letter...I didn't know if I was going to survive her running away. I was terrified to think of all the things that could have happened to her.

LILLAS. I know, Mama. I'll never forgive Vernie for worrying you like she did.

MAMA. You mustn't feel that way, Lilla'. You sisters must always stick together. LaVerne didn't know she would hurt me...she just felt like seeing Alaska and off she went.

LILLAS. But, to not tell us? To just go off like that? That was cruel.

MAMA. *(SHE rises to go to the sink.)* What would I do without you, dear girl? You're the sensible one. Happily married, settled, with a good husband and a beautiful daughter.

*(Suddenly the door flies open. **VIOLET** bursts in over laden with suitcases and her gear. She is big city chic with fancy clothes and the latest hairstyle.)*

VIOLET. I'M HOME!

MAMA. For goodness sakes, child, you scared me half to death! What are you doing here? We were just reading your letter.

VIOLET. Good, you got it. Philip's gone for good and I just had to get away. *(She dumps her luggage in a corner.)* Aren't you glad to see me?

LILLAS. Really, Vi. Why didn't you call? *(Beat.)* How long before you take him back this time?

VIOLET. It's final this time. He was gambling every penny we made at the restaurant. He just wouldn't quit, Mama. As for you, Lillas Elizabeth, your sarcasm doesn't go unnoticed. But, we can't all have a steady, boring, husband like Richard, now can we?

LILLAS. How dare you! Richard is not...

MAMA. Now, girls, don't bicker. Sit down, Violet. Couldn't you reason with Phillip, dear?

VIOLET. I've reasoned with him for over fourteen years. He keeps promising he'll quit and then some dog or horse comes along and he can't resist. I'm sick of it.

LILLAS. Are you divorcing him?

VIOLET. Oh, yes, as soon as possible.... I've got some other, bigger news...

LILLAS. Where are the children?

VIOLET. I had to find them somewhere to live, temporarily. I couldn't do it all. I work in the bar all day, then hostess and manage in the restaurant at night. I boarded them out.

MAMA. *(Sputtering.)* You what!? Boarded them?

LILLAS. Your own children?

MAMA. I don't understand. What happened to the girl you had in to watch them?

VIOLET. Oh, that little twit! She ran off with some soldier. Anyway, I couldn't take care of the kids and run the business too.

MAMA. Then you should have sold the business.

VIOLET. Sell the business? The restaurant that I have put my life's blood into? Really, Mother, what a thing to say.

MAMA. I never heard of such a thing. A child of mine abandoning her own children. I'm ashamed of you, Violet.

VIOLET. Mama...don't say that. I'll get them back. It's only for six months.

LILLAS. Six months?! **MAMA.** Oh, my word!

MAMA. What did Doris and Jackie say? When you told them...when you left them.

VIOLET. Jackie was so sweet.... He took my face into his little hands and said, 'Don't worry, Mommy, I understand. I'll work hard for Mrs. Daley. I'll be here when you come for me.'

MAMA. Oh, my stars! *(Wiping her eyes with the bottom of her apron.)* ...And Doris?

VIOLET. Oh, you know her. She's thirteen and hates me anyway.

MAMA. Violet Marie, I don't know you anymore. Your children living with strangers...

VIOLET. I'm pregnant, Mama.

MAMA. Oh, but that's wonderful. Does Philip know?

VIOLET. No! You don't understand. I've met a wonderful man. It's his baby.

LILLAS. *(Aghast.)* My God, Vi!

MAMA. I don't understand. Philip's gone, and you're still married to him...

VIOLET. Not for long...

MAMA. And you're having a baby with...with...

VIOLET. Jay...William J. Woods.

LILLAS. What in the world are you thinking, Vi? Who is this guy?

VIOLET. None of your business, Lillas. I'm having this conversation with Mama.

LILLAS. You're right. I can't stand to hear any more of it. I'll be upstairs.

(LILLAS exits up the stairs. MAMA sits, dumbfounded, staring at her daughter.)

VIOLET. Now, Mama, don't look so shocked.

MAMA. But, Violet, I don't understand. When did all of this happen?

VIOLET. About three months ago. Phillip and I had this horrible fight about his gambling and I threw him out. He's been gone since then. I don't even know where he is.

MAMA. But, this man...this 'Jay' person...where did you meet him?

VIOLET. Oh, he's been a regular customer at the bar for a long time. He always flirted with me, but then so do most of my customers. I didn't think too much of it. Then one night Phillip and I were arguing in the back storeroom and I guess they could hear us out in the bar...I came back out and my eyes were all red from crying—I was so mad! Anyway, Jay noticed and said, 'Come on, we're going for a walk'. He took me by the elbow, grabbed my coat and walked me out.

MAMA. Well, I never...

VIOLET. Oh, Mama, he was so wonderful. We walked and talked for two hours. He was so understanding and sweet.

MAMA. But, who is he? What does he do for a living?

VIOLET. Like I told you, Mama., his name is William J. Woods, but he goes by Jay. He's in the Navy...a chief warrant officer. Oh, Mama, you should see him...he's this big Irishman—black hair and blue eyes...he's so handsome.

MAMA. And you're pregnant? Are you sure?

VIOLET. Yes, Mama, I'm sure. About seven weeks. We're so in love.

MAMA. But, how? I mean...you're married to another man.

VIOLET. *(Irrepressible in her new love, VIOLET. laughs.)*

VIOLET. Oh, the usual way, Mama.... We went camping up in the Sierras and there was this beautiful full moon...you felt like you could reach out and touch it. We tried to be careful...I didn't have my diaphragm with me...

MAMA. *(Shocked)* Violet, please...!

VIOLET. Sorry. Anyway, I lay there in Jay's arms and we looked at the moon and you know what he said?

MAMA. I dare not imagine.

VIOLET. He said, 'Vi, if we make a baby tonight, I hope her life is as beautiful as this moonlit night.' 'Her life', he said. He's sure it's a girl. It was so wonderful, I cried.

MAMA. Sounds just like an Irishman! Full of malarkey. *(Beat.)* I don't know, child. You're thirty-nine...is it safe, your having a baby at that age?

VIOLET. My doctor says it's a little old, but I'm healthy and the baby is doing fine.

MAMA. And what kind of father will this Jay person be...you met him in a bar. You met Phillip at a racetrack and look what happened.

VIOLET. Where else would I meet someone? I'm at my bar working sixteen hours a day.

MAMA. Oh, Violet... Well, what's done is done. What are your plans? Does he want to marry you?

VIOLET. Of course he wants to marry me! What a question. He is shipping out for two months—maneuvers, or something. When he gets back my divorce will be final and we'll get married. It'll all work out. You'll see, Mama.

(LILLAS enters from down the stairs. She is wearing her coat and hat. SHE crosses to MAMA and kisses her forehead.)

LILLAS. I best start back, Mama. I don't like to drive alone at night.

MAMA. I know, dear. Be careful, won't you?

VIOLET. Well. Don't you want to know the dirty details, Lilla'? Aren't you the least bit curious about my illicit affair?

LILLAS. It might surprise you, Vi, but no, I don't want the details. To board your own children out and run off with some sailor? My God, what are you thinking? Have you completely lost your mind?

VIOLET. You were listening!

LILLAS. I was not.

VIOLET. Were too. How did you know Jay's a sailor?

LILLAS. Your voice carries...

VIOLET. You were listening to every word, you big snoop.

LILLAS. I was not!

VIOLET. Were too.

MAMA. Girls, please!

VIOLET. But, Mama...she's always so sanctimonious! With her perfect husband, her perfect daughter...

LILLAS. What do you know?

MAMA. Girls! Stop it this instant!

LILLAS. I'm sorry, Mama.   **VIOLET.** Sorry...

LILLAS. I have to go. I'll call you in a couple of days. How long are you staying, Vi?

VIOLET. Don't know yet. A week? Two?

(LILLAS is at the door. MAMA follows her and closes the door after her. We hear a car pulling away a few moments later. MAMA turns back into the room.)

MAMA. Well, now, tell me all about this wonderful man, Jay? How does he feel about becoming an instant father?

VIOLET. Oh, he has a daughter by another marriage.... He's thrilled.

(LIGHTS fade.)

ACT II~Scene 2

(AT RISE: Fall. 1941. LILLAS and IVAH sit at the table set with teapot, tea cups, the remains of a meal. VIOLET, who is now obviously pregnant, and MAMA stand at the kitchen window, watching VIOLET's children playing outside. As THEY talk they turn to each other, then look out the window.)

VIOLET. How do you think the children seem, Mama?

MAMA. Doris is too quiet...and your son is too noisy. I don't believe boarding them did anybody any good.

IVAH. That's saying a mouth full.

VIOLET. *(VIOLET turns out to the room.)* Did anyone ask you, Ivah?

IVAH. Nope. Just the same, Mama's right...Jackie's changed. He used to be such a good little boy. And Doris? Whew! If looks could kill...

VIOLET. Oh, pish, Ivah, what do you know?

MAMA. I'm just worried about them, Violet.

VIOLET. I know.

(BOTH women turn away from the window. They have their arms around each other as they walk towards the table to join LILLAS and IVAH.)

VIOLET. I got them back as soon as I could. I even broke the six-month contract.

LILLAS. Vi, I don't mean to criticize but that sounds more like indentured servants than two kids being boarded out.

MAMA. Well, they're home now and that's all that matters. I'm sure they'll settle in. Not to worry, Violet.

LILLAS. Thank God they're back with you Vi.

LILLAS. Just give them lots of love and attention and everything will come right.

IVAH. When will the sale on the bar be final, Vi?

VIOLET. Soon. The lawyers have the paperwork to do, then it's final.

IVAH. Who'd you sell it to?

VIOLET. One of my regulars...he has a silent partner who put up some of the money. They cashed me out.

IVAH. I still can't believe you're selling. A few months ago nobody could have pried that bar out of your cold dead hands...

VIOLET. Well, a person's priorities change. I have Jay and the baby to think about now.

MAMA. I think you did the right thing. Coming home while Jay is gone. It's best that you and the children are here.

LILLAS. Speaking of bars, Vi, wait until you hear what happened to Ivah's Sandy at the tavern where she works.

VIOLET. What?

IVAH. *(To VIOLET.)* Well, you know how much Sandy wants a baby girl. It broke her heart when the doctor said no more children after the two boys.

MAMA. But, Ivah, really, to pass a baby over a tavern counter and just give her away...

VIOLET. What? What baby?

IVAH. While you were outside with Doris and Jack, I was telling Mama and Lilla' that last week, some drunken woman came into Sandy's tavern. She had a baby with her. Sandy began making over her, mostly because she was a baby girl. Sandy said the baby was so good. Quiet, never a peep out of her. After about an hour of drinking, the woman pushed the baby along the counter and told Sandy, 'You like her? You can have her!'

LILLAS. Did you ever hear of such a thing?

VIOLET. Wow!

LILLAS. Why does Sandy want to work in such a place? She should be home with her boys.

IVAH. Dennis' work's been slow. They can use the money and she likes to get out. The boys are in bed by the time she leaves for work.

VIOLET. Never mind that, what happened?

IVAH. The woman got off the bar stool, cool as you please, and started to walk out. Sandy tried to stop her. Followed her out of the place with the baby in her arms and pleaded with her not to leave the baby. The woman pulled away, staggered down the street. Sandy caught up with her and told her when she 'felt better' the next day, the woman could come back. That she'd find Sandy working there most nights...to come back and get her child. The woman muttered something about 'good riddance' and left.

MAMA. My stars. What is this world coming to?

LILLAS. Did the woman come back?

VIOLET. Does it sound like it, Lila'? You always have to have happily-ever-afters.

LILLAS. I do not.

VIOLET. Do too.

MAMA. Girls! So, what happened, Ivah?

IVAH. Nothing. The woman hasn't been back and it's been eight days now. I'm really worried about Sandy. What's going to happen to my daughter if and when this drunk comes back looking for her child. Meanwhile, Sandy is falling in love with this little girl.

MAMA. Have you seen her? The baby, I mean?

IVAH. *(Sighs and nods.)* Oh, my, she's just the cutest thing you ever saw. Blonde like Sandy with the biggest blue eyes.

LILLAS. How old is she?

IVAH. The doctor thinks about 18 months...just a guess. She's so adorable. So good, never fusses. Just looks up at you with those big eyes...so serious.

MAMA. Sounds like someone else in the family has fallen for this little tyke.

IVAH. I'd like to see the woman who wouldn't...unless, it was Violet.

VIOLET. You shut up! You don't know anything about me.

IVAH. I know enough...I know you got rid of your kids...

VIOLET. I did not! I've got them back...

IVAH. Now that you've got this new man good and hooked. Does he even know you've got two kids?

VIOLET. You shut up, Ivah. You don't know how hard it is.

IVAH. Really!

VIOLET. You and your fancy brick home, your fancy friends...

MAMA. Girls, girls...enough. I'm sure Violet did what she thought she had to do...

VIOLET. That's right, Mama.

IVAH. Uh-huh. What's good for Vi...that's all she cares about.

MAMA. Ivah, please...be quiet. That's an ugly thing to say about your sister.

IVAH. Well, it's true.

VIOLET. It's not true! Just because you have such a perfect life—

MAMA. Ivah! Violet! You are in my house. You are not too old to be sent to your rooms. Quiet!

LILLAS. Oh, Mama., they are never going to change. They'll still be at each other when they're in their eighties.

MAMA. I sincerely hope not. *(Beat.)* Go on with your story, Ivah. What does Dennis say?

IVAH. Oh, Dennis is fine. Nothing gets to him. He just shrugs and says, 'What's one more baby around?' You know him, whatever Sandy wants, he wants. Sandy's already painted the nursery walls and bought so many little pink dresses, the child can't possibly wear them all.

LILLAS. What do the boys think about all of this.

IVAH. Oh, Gary and Dee Dee think the sun rises and sets in their new little sister. She's got them wrapped around her little finger.

MAMA. Surely they can't go on like this—not knowing from day to day.

IVAH. We're all just tippy-toeing around waiting for that woman to come back.

MAMA. What's the next step?

IVAH. They're going to see a lawyer next week. Arthur recommended a colleague who specializes in adoptions. Arthur is certain that there are laws about abandonment and such...but it's not his area of the law. We're hoping the child will be made a ward of the court until Sandy and Dennis can adopt her.

VIOLET. What's the baby's name?

IVAH. The woman never said. So Sandy calls her Eve. She's decided that Eve's birthday will be the night her mother gave her to Sandy. She adores that child.

MAMA. I just hope Sandy and Dennis know what they're doing, Ivah. I hate to say it but this could end very badly.

IVAH. I know, Mama. I'm very worried. I don't think she would ever recover from it, if that woman comes back and tries to take Eve. Oh dear, listen to me. Even I act as though she were my granddaughter.

MAMA. Things like this have a way of sorting themselves out. *(Beat.)* Now! How about a story?

LILLAS. Oh, yes, please!

VIOLET. It's been ages since we've heard a story, Mama.

LILLAS. I know, the one about the potatoes.

MAMA. All right.

(ALL the girls pull up their chairs closer to MAMA..)

MAMA. In honor of Vernie, I will start with everyone's ages at the time: Jerry was nineteen; Eddie was seventeen; Earl was sixteen; Coy thirteen; Ivah was twelve; Violet, you were eleven...let's see, that would have made Lillas...

LILLAS. Fourteen...

MAMA. Yes, thank you dear...fourteen. And Vernie was seven. Eddie and Jerry were with your father in the woods. I had gone to town to see if your father had sent money to the post office for us. He was working in Hoquiam, clear cutting cedar for a man.

MAMA. The man hadn't paid Papa on time so we were in very desperate times. We couldn't charge a penny more at Anderson's Food Emporium...

IVAH. Oh! Remember Abner Anderson? What a creep! And what'd he play?

VIOLET. The violin... **LILLAS.** The piccolo...?

IVAH. Eeeow...he had pimples everywhere...

MAMA. *(Pointedly.)* So, as I was saying...

LILLAS. Excuse us, Mama. **VIOLET.** Sorry...

IVAH. I haven't thought of Abner Pimpleface, in years!

MAMA. As I was saying...I couldn't possibly show myself at Anderson's without paying something on the bill. Before I went to town, I started a big skillet of fried potatoes and onions, and put it to the back of the stove. That and that alone was to be our dinner.

MAMA. You children were to stay in doors and I left you to play cards while I was gone.

VIOLET. And, Ivah, being the greedy gut that she is to this day, ate all the potatoes...

IVAH. DID NOT!

VIOLET. Did so!

LILLAS. Let Mama finish...

MAMA. Well, unbeknownst to the rest of you, Ivah got hungry and started sneaking potatoes out of the pan. By the time I returned home, most of everyone's supper was gone.

(Everyone knows the story, told time-and-again, but THEY still ask the questions.)

LILLAS. So what did you do next, Mama?

MAMA. I told you all that until the guilty party came forward and admitted to eating our supper that none of you could call me 'Mama'. And if you did call me 'Mama', I would ignore you.

VIOLET. So then, we six kids would catch Ivah alone and take her out in the woods behind the house...

LILLAS. And we'd beat her up until she promised to go to you, Mama, and confess.

MAMA. But, as soon as Ivah got away from you, she would run back to the house and stick to me like molasses...

VIOLET. She had to 'cause if we caught her alone, it was another beating...

LILLAS. That was the worst punishment you could have ever given us...I know, it killed me not to be able to call you 'Mama'.

VIOLET. So, come on, Ivy...we're all grown women here, with children of our own. 'Fess up...you ate all those potatoes, didn't you.

MAMA. Oh, child, leave her alone. It was so long ago...

IVAH. I earned those spuds...all the beatings you gave me.

VIOLET. Ah ha! So it was you!?

IVAH. What's the harm? Mama got Papa's money the very next day.

VIOLET. And you call me selfish!

IVAH. 'Cause you are...

VIOLET. Am not!

IVAH. Are too!

MAMA. Girls!

ACT II~SCENE 3

(AT RISE: Early afternoon, December 7, 1941. LAVERNE has just arrived home. MAMA is alone in the kitchen. The table is set for the mid-day meal. VIOLET is upstairs napping. The three girls are out in the barn seeing to the chickens and the milk cow. The radio is on, with low volume.)

MAMA. *(MAMA crosses to the kitchen door, opens it and calls out.)* GIRLS! Girls, dinner's ready.

LILLAS. *(Offstage. Yells back from the barn.)* We'll be right there Mama. We're almost finished.

MAMA. Come in while it's still hot.

(MAMA turns back into the room. Returning to the stove, she begins to dish up food. A few beats later LILLAS and IVAH, joined by LAVERNE, come through the door. LAVERNE has grown into a raw boned, pioneer woman. Lean as a whip, her skin is weathered by sun and wind. As the girls enter, they are laughing and pushing like teenagers. LAVERNE is carrying a basket with eggs. LILLAS has a pail of milk.)

LAVERNE. *(Brushing at the front of her flannel shirt.)* You didn't have to squirt me with the milk, Ivy! Now I'm all wet.

IVAH. It was an accident, I was aiming at the cat. Besides, that'll teach you to throw eggs!

MAMA. Get washed up girls, then sit down. Vernie, you can put those eggs in the cold chest, in the pantry.

LAVERNE. *(SHE steps into a pantry just off the kitchen and opens a cabinet door.)* Yes, Mama.

MAMA.   I declare, child, I can't believe it's you. All grown up, a regular pioneer woman living in the wilds of Alaska. Where did my baby disappear to?

> (*LILLAS sets the pail of milk on the floor and covers it with a clean cloth. As the GIRLS cross toward the sink to wash their hands EVERYONE's attention is caught by the urgency of the radio announcer's voice.*)

IVAH.   What was that?...What's he saying?

> (*MAMA hurries to turn up the volume on the radio.*)

LILLAS.   Did he say 'bomb'?...
MAMA.   Hush, girls...listen...
RADIO VOICE.   (*In the middle of the announcement.*)   ...bombed Pearl Harbor this morning...Initial reports are just coming in...

> (*EVERYONE begins to talk over the radio.*)

IVAH.   What!?
LILLAS.   <u>Our</u> Pearl Harbor?...in Hawaii?
MAMA.   I don't understand, we're not at war with anybody...
LAVERNE.   They must-a gotten it wrong...
IVAH.   (*In a loud voice, slapping the top of the radio and speaking to the radio.*) WHAT?! Who attacked?
MAMA.   Shhh! Violet is resting upstairs...I don't want her to hear.
RADIO VOICE.   To repeat this news bulletin for those of you that have just tuned in...I regret to report that the Japanese Air Force and Navy conducted a dawn bombing raid on our ships anchored in Pearl Harbor...Torpedoes are responsible for heavy damage...Hickam Field was also hit.... Stay tuned for updates as we receive them...

LaVERNE. What's Vi got to do with this?

IVAH. The Japs? They snuck in and bombed us?

LILLAS. The story's got to be wrong. Don't they have a delegate in Washington signing peace treaties? I don't understand...I've got to call Richard.

(LILLAS rushes off to make the call.)

LaVERNE. *(In a loud, excited voice.)* Those goddamn sneaky sonsabitches. Who can trust 'em?

MAMA. Shush. You'll wake Violet.

IVAH. Oh, my God. Violet! Jay's out there somewhere. What are we going to tell her?

MAMA. I don't know.

LaVERNE. Who's Jay?

(LILLAS comes back.)

LILLAS. Busy. I can't get through.

LaVERNE. Who's Jay?

MAMA. What's the name of his ship?

LaVERNE. *(Frustrated at being ignored again like the baby of the family.)* WHO'S JAY?

IVAH. Vi's latest.

LILLAS. The father of the child Vi's carrying.

MAMA. We haven't had time to tell you.

LaVERNE. Vi's knocked up?

IVAH. That about sums it up.

MAMA. LaVerne Louise! What a thing to say!

LAVERNE. Well, tell all. Where's Phillip in all this? I thought he was outta the picture. Where are Vi's kids? Jeez, I came home just in time.

LILLAS. Phillip's gone. Vi boarded her kids out somewhere for awhile but they're back here now and Vi's *(with a pointed look at LAVERNE's vulgarity.)* expecting in March.

LAVERNE. Who is this Jay guy?

IVAH. A sailor.

LAVERNE. *(Starts to giggle then laughs out loud.)* A...sailor...Oh, my God, leave it to Vi.

MAMA. It's not funny at all, LaVerne.

LAVERNE. *(Trying to get herself under control.)* I'm sorry, Mama. But, Vi puts me in the shade. *(Chuckling.)* Did she bother to get married? This makes what...number three?

MAMA. That first one didn't count and you know it...it was annulled.

IVAH. Oh, it counted, Mama. *(Counting on her fingers.)* Ricky, Phillip and now Jay. Yep, that's three.

LILLAS. *(Bringing them back to the horrible news.)* What are we going to tell her, Mama?

MAMA. I don't know...I'm afraid for the baby... *(A door slams off and we hear footsteps on the stairs.)* Shhh... Violet's coming down.

VIOLET. *(VIOLET enters from the stairs and sees LAVERNE for the first time.)* Vernie! My God, is it you? *(Turns to MAMA.)* Is it really Vernie?

MAMA. Yes, it is...all grown up.

VIOLET. *(Rushes to LAVERNE and hugs her.)* Welcome home! When did you get here? Give your big sister a kiss.

LAVERNE. *(Hugs her back and pats her tummy.)* Yeah, big sister is right! What'cha got in there...triplets?

VIOLET. *(Patting her stomach proudly.)* No, just one last time we checked. When did you get here?

LAVERNE. Just a couple of hours ago...you were sleeping.

VIOLET. Yeah, I seem to be doing a lot of that lately. My gosh, look at you...Alaska agrees with you.

(BOTH girls cross back to the table.)

Any tea left, Mama?
MAMA. Let me make fresh.

(MAMA rises and kisses VIOLET's forehead. SHE then crosses to the sink to make fresh tea. While it steeps, MAMA sits at the table.)

VIOLET. So, Vernie, how's Alaska? How's Milo? His name's Milo, right? Mama says he's a woodsman like Papa.

(EVERYONE is silent. LAVERNE looks at MAMA.. VIOLET nervously touches her hair.)

What? ...What's up? Why's everyone staring at me? Is my hair a mess?
MAMA. Violet, we have some news...
LILLAS. We don't want you to get upset.
IVAH. You have the baby to think about...
VIOLET. *(In a whisper.)* My kids...?
MAMA. No! Oh, my Lord, no. They're fine. They're having a fine old time with Sandy's kids.
VIOLET. What then? *(Beat.)* ...Jay...? *(No one speaks.)* It's Jay. *(More desperate.)* Isn't it? Tell me... Why won't you speak?

(LILLAS puts her arm around VIOLET. MAMA takes her hand.)

LILLAS. Now, Vi, it concerns Jay...but we don't know anything for sure...

(VIOLET pushes them off and jumps up. Looking at their faces, she knows it's bad. She rushes for the door, hysterical.)

VIOLET. JAY! JAY! I've got to go to him...

(IVAH and LILLAS jump up and rush to VIOLET, catching her before she bolts out the door. VIOLET goes limp and starts crying, the sisters bring her back to the table and sit. MAMA has gone to the sink for fresh tea and brings the pot back to the table.)

VIOLET. *(Looking at MAMA.)* Tell me...he's dead, isn't he.
LAVERNE. No, no...we don't know...
MAMA. *(Smoothing VIOLET's hair.)* Now, Baby, we don't know anything for sure and what we do know isn't much. But, this morning...the radio said that the Japansese bombed Pearl Harbor...
VIOLET. *(Leans over, wrapping her arms around her stomach, moaning.)* Oh, no...no...
IVAH. Do you know where Jay's ship was going? Where he is?
VIOLET. *(In a tiny voice.)* Pearl...
LILLAS. Oh, no.
IVAH. Oh, Vi... **LAVERNE.** Damn!
MAMA. Wait, girls. Let's not jump to bad conclusions. Jay was on his way to Pearl...that's doesn't mean he's there yet.
VIOLET. How bad is it? Did they get any of our ships? Did our guys shoot them down? *(Looks MAMA. in the eye.)* How bad, Mama?

MAMA. The radio said... (Sighs.) It sounds pretty bad, dear. But we just don't know yet. Nobody does. It just happened. Do you know the name of Jay's ship?
VIOLET. No. Yes. I can't think...
LILLAS. Try.
VIOLET. The Tennessee, I think.
LILLAS. Good girl. Let me try Richard again.
VIOLET. *(Still in shock.)* Richard?
LILLAS. Yes, he might know something. He may hear more than we are getting on the radio...
VIOLET. Yes! Please call him, Lilla...

(LILLAS. exits.)

VIOLET. Mama, turn the radio up...maybe they'll mention Jay's ship.
LAVERNE. Maybe you shouldn't...
MAMA. Are you sure, dear?
VIOLET. Yes, please. I have to know.

(IVAH. goes over to the radio and turn the volume up. A tinny, Edward R. Murrow-type voice is speaking.)

RADIO VOICE. ...This just in...We have a preliminary list of ships hit in the infamous dawn attack on our Navy by Japan A recap for those of you just tuning in...At dawn this morning the Japanese Air Force and Navy attacked us at Pearl Harbor. In spite of Japanese delegates attending a conference in our capital this week, Jap bombers and fighters swooped over Honolulu and dropped bombs on our naval ships lying peacefully at anchor. Bombers also hit Hickam Field but we have no details on damage or casualties at Hickam. We have been given an unofficial list of battleships hit, but we caution our listeners, this list is incomplete and as we have noted before, completely unofficial. The ships in harbor were the: USS

Pennsylvania Utah, West Virginia. The flagship of the Pacific Fleet, the USS California was also in harbor. The USS Maryland and the USS Tennessee. All are reported hit. No report on casualties is available at this time...Just in! Dateline: The White House...The United States has declared war on Japan and Germany. We will broadcast more information as we receive it after this important message...

> *(A commercial for Bon Ami cleanser comes on and IVAH. turns the volume down. As soon as VIOLET hears the name, "Tennessee", she begins to weep.)*

LAVERNE. Damned Japs!

MAMA. Now, Vi, that doesn't mean Jay was on board. We don't know anything at this point.

VIOLET. He's dead...I know it...

IVAH. No, he's not...come on, you've got to be brave...think about the baby.

> *(LILLAS comes back in. VIOLET looks at her. LILLAS shakes her head.)*

LILLAS. I got through to Richard's office but they are all in meetings. I left a message to call me as soon as possible.

Did the radio say anything new?

IVAH. Jay's ship, the Tennessee, is at Pearl.

IVAH. It's been hit but we don't know how bad.

LILLAS. *(Goes to Violet and embraces her.)* Oh, Vi, I am so sorry. Richard will find out something for us. I'm sure Jay is all right.

LAVERNE. *(False bravado.)* Sure, kiddo, our guys are tough...and our sailors are the toughest, in spite of what the Marines say.

VIOLET. Mama, what will I do? The baby...and now, if Jay's dead...what's to become of me...?

MAMA. *(MAMA takes her in her arms as she did when VIOLET was a baby and croons to her.)* You're going to do just fine, sweetheart. Aren't you my brave one? You will always have a home here with us. I don't want you to worry when we don't know which way is up...Jay's not gone...you'll see...

ACT II~SCENE 4

(AT RISE: Five days later. LILLAS and MAMA sit at the table. VIOLET comes down the stairs. She looks unkept and haggard.)

VIOLET. *(Standing at the foot of the stairs.)* Did I hear the telephone? Did Richard call?
LILLAS. Yes, he called while you were resting. He still hasn't heard anything.
VIOLET. What's taking so long? It's been five days... *(VIOLET's voice gets more shrill with her panic.)* Why can't anyone tell us anything?
MAMA. *(Goes to VIOLET and leads her back to the table.)* Now, Violet, I don't want you to worry. We should hear something very soon... Don't you think so, Lillas?
LILLAS. Yes, it's such a good sign that we haven't received any telegrams. I have so many friends, at home, that are getting them. *(Shaking her head.)* What a way to find out your husband or son or brother has been lost.

(There is a loud knock at the front door. MAMA starts to rise.)

LILLAS. Sit, Mama. I'll go.

(LILLAS exits left to the front door.)

MAMA. Who on earth can that be? No one we know comes to the front door.

(VIOLET doesn't answer, but just stares into her lap. LILLAS enters, hiding her hands behind her.)

LILLAS. Mama, could you come here a minute? I want to show you something.
MAMA. What? *(Beat.)* Why, Lillas you're as white as a sheet. Whatever's the matter?
VIOLET. *(Looks up at this. SHE jumps up.)* What's wrong, Lilla'?
LILLAS. Nothing. *(Beat.)* Mama...
VIOLET. What're you hiding? It's Jay, isn't it?

(LILLAS brings her hands from behind her. In her hand is the dreaded, yellow telegram envelope.)

LILLAS. I'm sorry, Vi.
MAMA. Oh, no...
VIOLET. *(Shocked beyond tears, VIOLET is deadly calm.)* May I have it please.
LILLAS. *(Crosses to her and hands her the envelope.)* I am so sorry...

(VIOLET walks to the kitchen table and sits. LILLAS and MAMA start to sit down with her.)

VIOLET. No, I'd like to be alone...

MAMA. Oh, honey, do you think you should...?
VIOLET. Please, Mama.

> *(BOTH women exit towards the front of the house, but don't go far. VIOLET methodically tears the envelope opens, unfolds the thin paper and reads. VIOLET screams and burst into tears. The telegram falls lifelessly from her hand. VIOLET has crossed her arms on the table, puts her head down and seemingly cries inconsolably.)*

MAMA. *(Rushing back into the kitchen with LILLAS. SHE takes VIOLET into her arms.)* Violet, my poor child...it will be all right...don't...you'll hurt the baby.

> *(LILLAS picks up the telegram and reads it to herself. When she lifts her head she is grinning. At the same time, VIOLET raises her head. She is crying and laughing with joy.)*

VIOLET. He's alive...he's safe...
MAMA. What? Jay...he's alive?
VIOLET. *(Motions to LILLAS.)* Read it.
LILLAS. Vi, darling. STOP. I am okay. STOP. My ship lightly damaged. STOP. Letter to follow. STOP. I love you. STOP. Jay
MAMA. Merciful heavens...he's safe.
VIOLET. *(Tears subsiding, she laughs.)* Jay told me...he said he would never leave me, not really...he would be back...

> *(Loud knocking, but at the kitchen door. ALL three women pale and stare at each other.)*

LILLAS. My God, now what?

(MAMA rises and looks out the window over the sink. She is visibly relieved when she turns back.)

MAMA. It's just Henry, the postman. Sometimes, he saves me a walk out to the road. Stops by for a chat.

VIOLET. *(Fussing with her hair.)* I can't see anyone now, Mama....

LILLAS. Let me go, I'll get rid of him. *(LILLAS goes to the door and opens it just a crack.)* Hello, Mr. Connelly...No, Mama is upstairs just now...Yes, thanks so much for bringing the mail....Bye, now.

(SHE closes the door and hands the mail to MAMA. MAMA flips through it and finds an `airmail' envelope with a FPO return address.)

MAMA. Oh, my stars! It's for you, Vi. It's from Jay.

LILLAS. My word, both on the same day?

MAMA. Here, darling...

VIOLET. *(A pause.)* I'm afraid.

MAMA. I'm sure it's all good news. Best way to find out is to open it.

VIOLET. It's from Jay. He's still at Pearl. *(SHE looks through the letter.)* But what are all these blacked out parts?

LILLAS. That's the censors. Richard says all the mail from Europe looks like that.

MAMA. Do you want to read it aloud to us, child?

VIOLET. Yes, of course. He writes...

'My darling Vi. I sent a telegram saying that I am all right but it is such a mess here right now, I can't trust that you are getting anything from me. I hope you and the baby are okay. I am sorry for the worry you must have felt when you heard about us getting bombed here at Pearl. Those Japs really blasted us. I was one of the lucky ones and had shore leave that weekend so I was sleeping in the barracks. Not so lucky for a lot of guys. The barracks got strafed a little but nothing serious. The Japs were going for our planes. They got-CENSORED of our planes before we could get them up in the air. I can't tell you much about where I am or where we are going. The censors are pretty strict about what we can write about in our letters home. But, let me tell you, we are chasing the Japs all over the-CENSORED We have new orders and we are heading for-CENSORED. The-CENSORED is in dry dock...'

(*VIOLET interjects here.*) He's probably talking about the Tennessee.

'...so I have a new ship. Being a warrant officer really pays off because I can just about get any duty I want so I got a berth on the-CENSORED. Sorry, can't tell you everything, but remember what we talked about before I left... I will try to get some information to you that way. We are not leaving warm waters. We are taking the war to the Japs' front door, believe you me! How are you feeling? Is the baby okay? I am so sorry we didn't get married before I shipped out. I thought I would be back by now and still have plenty of time before the baby comes for this old sailor to find home port. HA.HA. Guess we shouldn't have left anything to chance.'

(*VIOLET starts to choke up when she sees what he has written.*)

'But, remember this always, you are the love of my life and I will come home to you and the little squirt no matter how long this war lasts. Remember that night with the moon so full, what I said to you, ...when we...'

(*VIOLET looks up at her sisters and mother, blushing.*) Well, then the rest is kinda private...   (*VIOLET closes the letter and tucks it into her pocket.*) I'll finish it later.

MAMA. *(Looking through the mail.)* Well, my stars, here's a letter from Eddie. *(Opening it she reads aloud.)*

> 'Dearest Ma, how are you? I am fine. I have some news but I don't want you to worry or be upset.'

LILLAS. Oh, oh.   **VIOLET.** Mama...

MAMA. *(MAMA continues to read.)*

> 'Mama, I've re-enlisted. I couldn't stand it; everyone is joining up... The recruiting offices are packed with guys wanting to get into the fight. I had to wait four hours just to get to the front of the line. The bad news is I can't get home for a visit. What with all my previous time in the service they are shipping me out in two days...'

(MAMA begins to cry quietly.) Oh, no, my baby boy...not again. Here, Lillas, you finish it...

LILLAS. *(Continues to read.)*

> '...shipping me to France where I will help with the invasion. I can't tell you more than that because of the censors. I know that you won't approve, Ma, but since we declared war on the Japs and the Germans, I just have to do this. I gotta run for now. Tell the girls hello for me..... You're still my best girl. I send my love to you all. Your son, Eddie'

Oh, Mama, don't cry...it will be all right. Eddie's been in the military all those years, he knows how to keep safe.

VIOLET. Sure, Mama, not a scratch in all those years. He'll be fine.

MAMA. I've lost one son to a war. I don't think I could bear losing another.

VIOLET. You are not going to lose Eddie...

MAMA. No, I have a bad feeling...he was spared the first time...this is tempting fate, somehow.

LILLAS. Now, Mama, don't say things like that out loud...

MAMA. *(Drying her eyes on her apron.)* Oh, I know I'm just being silly. Eddie is one of the finest soldiers ever...just look at all the medals and ribbons he has.

VIOLET. That's it, keep your chin up...you've got a new grandchild to help me with. And Jay's safe...everything will turn out fine, Mama. This war won't last now that we're in it. Everyone will come home safe, you'll see.

MAMA. Oh, child, let's hope God is listening...

ACT II~SCENE 5

(AT RISE: One month later. LILLAS and IVAH are sitting at the table. MAMA and VIOLET are at the sink washing up the dishes.)

IVAH. *(In the middle of a story.)* ...so Sandy said that around one in the morning in walks that woman who gave Eve to Sandy. She's drunker than the first time, if that's possible.

LILLAS. Did Sandy have the papers with her?

IVAH. Oh, yes. The attorney told her to keep them with her in case the mother showed up. So Sandy's been keeping them in the cash register at work.

VIOLET. What happened?

IVAH. Sandy asked her if she remembered giving Eve to her. The woman said, 'Sure, I was glad to get rid of the little brat.' She didn't even ask Sandy how the baby was or anything.

MAMA. Heartless!

LILLAS. Did Sandy get her signature on the papers?

IVAH. Not right at first. Sandy explained to her that she would like to adopt Eve but in order to do that; the woman would have to release her parental rights to Eve. She showed the papers to her. Then, and you are not going to believe this part...the woman asked Sandy what it was worth to her.

MAMA. Oh my stars.

VIOLET. What a worthless... **LILLAS.** What kind of mother...?

IVAH. Well, Sandy didn't know what to say. She told her that she didn't have much money in her purse but she was welcome to all of it. Then Jake, Sandy's boss, stepped in and asked the woman how fifty bucks sounded. He opened the till and took out the money.

IVAH. The woman looked Jake dead in the eye and said, "a hundred". Jake stared her down and said, "Fifty or nothing". The woman grabbed Sandy's pen and signed on the spot! Jake and Mary Louise witnessed it for Sandy. The woman grabbed the money from Jake and ran out the door. She was in such a hurry, she didn't even pay for her drinks.

MAMA. So the adoption can go through now?

IVAH. It will be final in six months.

MAMA. It was meant to be.

LILLAS. That's wonderful, Ivy.

IVAH. You just can't imagine how relieved I am...Sandy adores that little girl.

LILLAS. Mama.... *(Looks at her sisters and mother.)* Mama, I need to speak with you in private.

IVAH. What's up?

LILLAS. Nothing.... I just need to talk to Mama.

VIOLET. So talk.

LILLAS. Can you two go outside or something?

IVAH. No. I want to hear. **VIOLET.** Why do we—

LILLAS. Mama!

MAMA. All right, girls...run down to the barn and get me some cream for the gravy.

VIOLET. Oh, Mama., why can't we hear?

IVAH. Yeah, we share everything. What's so secret, Lilla'?

LILLAS. We don't share everything! And this is none of your business.

VIOLET. Mama... **IVAH.** Lilla', you're not the boss...

MAMA. Ivah, did I not ask you two to run down to the barn for me?

IVAH. Yes, Ma'am.

MAMA. And find something to do for at least fifteen minutes.

IVAH. O...kay. **VIOLET.** Okay.

(VIOLET and IVAH exit; grumbling.)

MAMA. *(With a big sigh.)* I declare you girls can act so childish. *(Beat.)* Now! What can I help with?

LILLAS. Maxine's pregnant.

MAMA. Oh, no. Oh, I'm so sorry. Are you sure? How did this happen? *(LILLAS gives MAMA an arch look.)* Well, of course, I know how it happened, but I didn't know you were allowing her to date...

LILLAS. We weren't. She's only allowed to go in a group of kids.

MAMA. Oh dear.

LILLAS. Yes indeed. Funny how history repeats itself.

MAMA. How far along?

LILLAS. Two months. She's been hiding it from us...scared to death.

MAMA. Do you know who the boy is?

LILLAS. Yes, but the boy's parents won't talk to us. He's only sixteen. The moment we told them they sent their son away.

MAMA. Oh my. What will you do?

LILLAS. I'm going to keep the child as my own, Mama.

MAMA. Oh, my dear. You're forty-what?

LILLAS. Forty-two.

MAMA. Yes, forty two. No one is going to believe you are pregnant. How are you going to manage it?

LILLAS. I won't have Maxine's life ruined like mine.

MAMA. *(Shocked.)* Lillas Sophia! What a thing to say! Your life wasn't ruined. You have Richard, a good marriage, you've traveled the world, you have two beautiful daughters.

LILLAS. All someone else's choices, Mama. Oh, I'm not saying I don't love Richard. I do. But, I didn't get to choose for myself. Because of one stupid decision, I had to get married. I travel with Richard because of his job and because if I didn't, I'd never see him.

MAMA. But, Lillas...

LILLAS. No one has ever asked me what I would like to do with my life. It was just assumed that I wanted to be a wife and mother.

MAMA. That's not fair, Lillas. When you came home, expecting Phyllis, you were already married. I didn't have an opportunity to advise you.

LILLAS. I know, Mama, and you were wonderful to me. I'm not blaming anyone but myself. I was so young, so in love with love. But, I had dreams too.

MAMA. I know, dear.

LILLAS. I mean, look at Vi.

MAMA. *(Sardonically.)* Yes, look at Vi.

LILLAS. I know she's made mistakes, Mama. But she went after her dreams, fulfilled them. Nothing seems to get in her way. I want that for Maxine. I don't want all of her choices taken away from her by becoming a mother at fifteen.

MAMA. What does Maxine say?

LILLAS. She's confused. She's scared. God, Mama, she's so young...she's my baby.

MAMA. How will you make people believe that you had a child?

LILLAS. Richard and I have talked it all out. He has an opportunity to work in New Delhi for at least a year. If he takes the job they won't draft him...he'll be exempt.

MAMA. India...? So far away...

LILLAS. It's perfect timing. We can go away, all of us, before Maxine starts to show and when we come home, we'll have a new baby. It will never cross anyone's mind that it isn't Richard's and mine.

MAMA. Your sisters will have to be told. I won't keep that big a secret from them, Lillas.

LILLAS. I know, Mama. I wouldn't ask you to. I just needed to talk to you first.

LILLAS. Ivah and Violet will have a heyday with this bit of news...

MAMA. I think you'll be surprised...they can be wicked but they are rarely cruel, dear. Does Phyllis know?

LILLAS. No, not yet. She's going to climb all over her baby sister when she finds out. You know Phyllis, so together in whatever she does.

MAMA. Phyllis may be disappointed but she'll rally around when it comes to family. *(Beat.)* How soon will you leave?

LILLAS. Oh, not for a couple of months. And, of course, everything depends on the war in Europe.

(The kitchen door opens and VIOLET peeks around the door. IVAH's head is right above VIOLET's.)

VIOLET. Can we come in?

IVAH. Can we sound the all–clear?

LILLAS. Yeah, we're finished.

MAMA. Who wants tea?

VIOLET. No thanks, Mama.

IVAH. Maybe later. Come on, Lilla', dish the dirt.
LILLAS. Mama.! See what I mean?
IVAH. Whad' I say?
MAMA. Girls... Sit down and be respectful. Lillas is in trouble and I expect you to support her. Just as she has supported you, *(MAMA gives both girls a hard look.)* many times.
IVAH. Sorry, Mama.   **VIOLET.** Yeah...
MAMA. Lillas, go ahead. Tell them.
LILLAS. Maxine's pregnant.
VIOLET. What!?   **IVAH.** Holy Christopher!
VIOLET. But, Lilla', she's just a baby. What is she now, fourteen? What happened?
LILLAS. Just fifteen.
IVAH. Is she even suppose to be dating?
LILLAS. She and a boy got too serious...and, well, now there's a baby.
VIOLET. You were letting her date? This young?
LILLAS. I wasn't 'letting her date'. She wasn't suppose to until she turned sixteen. The only time I ever saw this boy was with a bunch of other kids.
IVAH. Well, they obviously didn't stay with the bunch...
LILLAS. Thank you very much, Ivah!
IVAH. What? I just made the observation...
MAMA. Try to be more supportive, Ivah.
IVAH. I am! I just asked...
LILLAS. Oh, for Godssake, Ivah, shut up!
VIOLET. What are you going to do, Lilla'?
LILLAS. We're keeping the baby, of course. But, I don't want Maxine to have to marry and start raising a family. She's just a child herself. Besides, the boy has been shipped off, God knows where.

IVAH. Oh nice! Isn't that typical? Let me guess, the boy's parents, all of a sudden, don't know you? Right?

MAMA. I'm afraid that's true.

VIOLET. Men!

LILLAS. So, Richard has been offered a posting to New Delhi...

IVAH. India?? **VIOLET.** India!

LILLAS. Yes...

VIOLET. But, there's a war on...

MAMA. Yes, we know, Violet. Go on Lillas.

LILLAS. And if he takes the post, he will be exempt from the draft. By the time we return the baby will be at least nine months old and we will say it's mine. No one the wiser.

IVAH. Lillas, you have got to be crazy as a loon to go to India when half the world is at war. Where is your brain?

LILLAS. Mama—

MAMA. Girls, listen to me.

MAMA. This is Richard's and Lillas' decision. They wouldn't send Richard to a post that was unsafe. Lillas wants Maxine to have a chance in life...she certainly won't have many choices if she takes on a baby at fifteen. I expect you girls to keep this to yourselves and support Lilla' in whatever way you can. Do I make myself clear?

VIOLET. Yes, Mama. **IVAH.** Yes, but—

MAMA. No buts, Ivah! Do I make myself clear on this subject?

IVAH. Yes, Ma'am.

VIOLET. India. You're very brave, Lilla'.

LILLAS. I'm not brave at all. In fact, I'm scared to death. But, we'll all be together and Maxine will have a second chance to chase her dreams.

MAMA. It was meant to be, I guess. *(Taking LILLAS' hand.)* But, my darling daughter, promise you'll be careful...it's so far away...

ACT II~SCENE 6

(AT RISE: One month later. IVAH, LAVERNE, VIOLET and MAMA are sitting around the kitchen table. It is a celebration of some kind, a large cake with candles, wrapping paper, dishes, and tea pot. LILLAS, standing at the sink, wears a maternity smock but her tummy is board flat. VIOLET is seven months pregnant now. As the scene opens they are ALL laughing and talking.)

MAMA. *(Basking.)* All my girls home again. My world is complete.

VIOLET. How was the train ride down Vernie?

LAVERNE. Not too bad. Snow on the tracks outside Fairbanks but it was only a two hour delay.

IVAH. Milo was okay with you coming?

LAVERNE. Oh, Gosh, yes. He's in the woods, cutting. Hardly knows I'm gone. Besides, I wasn't about to miss seeing my big sister off to the wilds of... *(Pronouncing it English-style as a joke.)* ...In-ja! *(Beat.)* When is Papa getting here?

MAMA. Sometime tomorrow. When he called he said not to let *(Smiling at LILLAS.)* you get away until he got home.

LILLAS. I couldn't possibly leave without kissing him goodbye.

VIOLET. Daddy's girl.

(LILLAS sticks her tongue out at VIOLET.)

IVAH. You look so hilarious in that maternity smock, Lilla. Do you think that you are fooling anyone?

LILLAS. This is my third baby shower. What do you think? Everyone is giving us combination going away parties and baby showers.

MAMA. How's Maxine feeling?

LILLAS. Oh, she's just fine. Healthy and not a sign of morning sickness. She isn't showing at all yet.

VIOLET. How is she taking to the idea that this baby will be raised as her sister or brother?

LILLAS. She seems all right...she was so afraid that she would have to give the baby up entirely. I've explained, as best I can, that no one must ever know that the baby is really hers and not mine. Especially the child. Maxine wants to go to college and she understands that this decision will allow her to go.

MAMA. It's going to be much harder once the baby is here.

LILLAS. I know, Mama. But we just have to take one thing at a time.

MAMA. I know, dear. I'm just afraid for all of you. There may come a day when Maxine finds herself resenting this secret. *(Beat.)* Oh, well, we just have to do the best we can. Have you picked out names?

LILLAS. Maxine picked out Sally Anne if it's a girl. And I like Edward Levi if it's a boy.

MAMA. *(Getting a little teary.)* Oh my. 'Edward' after your brother and 'Levi' for your Papa.

LILLAS. *(Smiling fondly.)* I thought that would make you happy, Mama.

LAVERNE. I like 'Sally'. It's sounds solid.

VIOLET. Don't ever tell your new niece you referred to her as 'solid'.

IVAH. When do you sail?

LILLAS. Next Monday. We take the train down to Los Angeles and board there.

MAMA. Oh, Lillas, I am going to miss you all so much. And I won't be there when the baby comes.

LILLAS. We're going to miss you too. All of you. But, it's a perfect solution to our problem and we'll be home before you know it, Mama.

VIOLET. Will you bring us each a sari, Lilla'? I want a red one.

LILLAS. Of course I will.   **LaVERNE.** What's a sari?

VIOLET. An Indian dress made of pure silk. You know, they kinda wrap around.

MAMA. Who wants more cake?

VIOLET. *(Holding her middle and laughing.)* Oooo... I couldn't eat another bite. My doctor would kill me if he knew I was eating cake.

IVAH. Mama tells us that Jay is coming home, Vi.

VIOLET. Yes! Isn't it the best news?

IVAH. How bad is his injury?

VIOLET. The fall broke his leg in three places.

IVAH. What happened?

VIOLET. They were out in very rough seas. He fell off a gangway ladder. They're sending him home to have surgery at the Veteran's Hospital in Seattle.

LILLAS. Will he have to go back?

VIOLET. I hope not. With any luck, the war will be over before the leg heals. *(Shows her crossed fingers and crosses her eyes at her sisters.)* I've got everything crossed.

IVAH. This damn war!

MAMA. No swearing, Ivah.

(Beat. EVERYONE is lost in their own personal thoughts about the World War that they are caught up in.)

VIOLET. Jay is so upset that this accident happened. I think he actually would've preferred to have a gunshot wound in a fight with the Japs. There's no understanding the way men think.

(Laughter.)

LILLAS. You know what I want more than anything, Mama?

MAMA. What's that, dear girl?

LILLAS. A story!

LAVERNE. Oh yes, a story!

MAMA. Are you girls ever going to grow out of being told stories?

VIOLET. Please, Mama....

IVAH. I know! The fish tank... **LAVERNE.** Oh, yes, that's a good one...

LILLAS. Yes! It's one of my favorites...

MAMA. Oh, all right...a story then. One summer, your Papa and I took you kids up to...

LAVERNE. Stop! You have to start the story with how old we all were...it's tradition, Mama. Start with me like you always do.

MAMA. *(Smiling fondly at LAVERNE.)* I forgot...well, let's see: you were four; Violet was six; Gladys was seven; Ivah and Coy were nine; Lillas. was eleven; and Earl was almost twelve; Eddie was thirteen; and Grace was fifteen. As I was saying, your Papa and I took you kids up to Olympia to the Aquarium at Nisqually Point. The older children stayed at home. Said it was too childish for them. It was somebody's birthday as I recall...

LAVERNE. It was mine.

IVAH. No it wasn't, twit, it was mine!

VIOLET. Yeah, Vernie, you were only four...how would you know?

IVAH. Yeah. Hush now! Let Mama tell...

MAMA. You're both wrong. It was Earl's birthday outing. We were going early because school was starting in a few weeks. Earl always hated that his outing could never be on his birthday.

VIOLET. Earl was such a whiner when he was little.

IVAH. He really hasn't changed much...

(ALL the sisters laugh.)

MAMA. Anyway, off we went for the day. We packed a picnic dinner and loaded everyone into the car.

IVAH. *(With a nostalgic sigh.)* Papa's old Packard.

VIOLET. *(Laughing.)* Remember that old thing? The paint was peeling off and it had no front fenders as I recall...

IVAH. ...but Papa said, 'it ran like a race horse' so why get rid of it?

VIOLET. That's Papa...waste not, want not.

LaVERNE. Then what, Mama?

MAMA. Well, off we went. When we got to the Aquarium, of course you older children wanted to go off on your own, so your Papa and I took you young ones with us and we all agreed to meet back at the entrance in time for our dinner. If I remember correctly, your sister, Grace, stayed with me to take care of you younger children and help with dinner. The Aquarium had the loveliest family area with picnic tables and tall shade trees. Well, later, I was just setting out the plates and the food, when you older ones came traipsing back...and you were all soaked to the skin...

(IVAH and LILLAS start to grin.)

Thank God it was summer, you would have caught your death. Anyway, your Papa asked you what you had been up to and Ivah, you said, 'Nothing, we've just been to the fish tanks. I guess they splashed us a lot'. Oh, butter wouldn't melt in your mouth, Ivah.

(IVAH grins wickedly.)

VIOLET. She always could tell the biggest whoppers...

IVAH. Uh-uh, you could...

LaVERNE. Hush up! Go on, Mama, what happened then?

MAMA. Well, by the time we had our picnic it was really time to start for home. The headlights weren't working on the Packard so we couldn't drive at night. About half way home, we had stopped by the side of the road so you children could Mama use the bushes. And as Eddie walked back to the car the lining in his pocket gave way and out of the bottom of his pant leg came all this money...fifty cent pieces, quarters, dimes, nickels...Well, you children didn't have any money so I knew something was up...your Papa and I made all of you empty your pockets right there on the side of the road. My stars, I think there was fifty dollars between the bunch of you.

VIOLET. Forty eight dollars and seventy cents, Mama... *(In hushed tones.)* They stole it!

IVAH. We didn't mean to steal it!

VIOLET. Did so.

IVAH. Did not!

LILLAS. Will you please let Mama. tell the rest of the story?

MAMA. So your Papa got a bag out of the car and collected up every cent. We sat you children down right there and got the whole story out of you.

LAVERNE. *(The story had been told many times.)* It was a wishing tank, wasn't it, Mama..

MAMA. Yes, child. People came to see the baby sharks in the tank and would throw coins in and make a wish. Then the money would be given to Children's Hospital.

LAVERNE. *(To the other girls.)* Ooo...you were in so much trouble.

IVAH. Well, gosh, Mama., we didn't know. We just thought it was a great game. To get past the vicious sharks and grab the money when they weren't looking. We thought the sharks would chew off our hands.

VIOLET. *(Grinning at IVAH.)* And let me guess who's idea this game was...

IVAH. Oh, shut up!

MAMA. Girls...

LAVERNE. Go on, Mama, what happened next?

MAMA. *(Looking straight at IVAH.)* I told the culprits that when we got home you would all go out in the yard and cut Mama your own personal switches. The next day you would get your punishment.

VIOLET. That was the worst...having to wait for the switching.

LaVERNE. Did they get to keep the money, Mama?

MAMA. Absolutely not. The next weekend your Papa had to drive them all the way back to the Aquarium. Ivah and Earl and Coy and Eddie had to give the money back and apologize to the owner.

IVAH. That was the worst punishment...the switch didn't even hurt compared to facing that man...

LaVERNE. Did Ivy have to apologize?

VIOLET. What'd the man do, Mama?

IVAH. Cured me of stealing forever...

MAMA. Looking very stern, he gave you kids a good talking to. But, as he turned to walk away, he gave your Papa a big wink...

(As LIGHTS fade and the play ends, EVERYONE is laughing and talking about another wonderful family story.)

CURTAIN

Also by
Trisha Sugarek...

Emma and the Lost Unicorn

The Exciting Exploits of an Effervescent Elf

Stanley the Stalwart Dragon

Please visit our website **bakersplays.com** for complete descriptions and licensing information.

OTHER TITLES AVAILABLE FROM BAKER'S PLAYS

EMMA AND THE LOST UNICORN

Trisha Sugarek

Fantasy / 4m, 5f, 6 additional speaking roles & additional non-speaking roles / Single set

Rainey, the unicorn, is a prince who has been banished to the forest for centuries by the warlock, Kodak. The prince can never return home unless someone solves more riddles than the warlock and discovers Kodak's secret weakness. A surprise twist ending makes this modern fable appealing to adults and children alike. Mythical creatures, scary henchmen, a warlock, queen, faeries, all co-habit an enchanted forest with giggles provided by a rhetorical owl and a naughty elf.

BAKERSPLAYS.COM

OTHER TITLES AVAILABLE FROM BAKER'S PLAYS

THE EXCITING EXPLOITS OF AN EFFERVESCENT ELF

Trisha Sugarek

Comedy / 9f, 2m, 2 either, with extras

Cheets, the irrepressible elf, saves Emma and the enchanted forest from certain destruction! Lord Hazard has employed Patsy, the Banana Spider, to keep Emma ensnared in her web while Hazard sells the forest to developers. Given his reputation for mischief, no one believes Cheets when he claims that he has found Emma because no one but Cheets can see her. Audience participation is encouraged, especially when Emma plays charades with Cheets to make herself understood. A stand alone sequel to *Emma and the Lost Unicorn*, new characters are introduced; Thomas, a sea turtle, nautical to his toes; Patsy, the spider, means well but cannot resist the tasty bugs supplied to her by Hazard. Rose and Lord Hazard, century old lovers, reunite. This fable contains greed, ecology, friendship, enduring love and justice.

www.ingramcontent.com/pod-product-compliance
Lightning Source LLC
Chambersburg PA
CBHW071839290426
44109CB00017B/1862